PREFACE

I didn't want to be a vet, but I loved drawing pictu
father encouraged me, and soon I was attemptin(
watercolours. He told me that one day I might be
teacher.

ACKNOWLEDGEMENTS

I am very grateful to Peter Forrester B.A. (Hons) for his advice and editing
help. I must also thank Jim Wight, B.V.M.S., M.R.C.V.S. for advice and
encouragement. Thanks also to Linda Forrester and Ruth Packer for
proofreading.

1

CONTENTS

Chapter One	Cornwall	5
Chapter Two	First Winter	15
Chapter Three	My Trial	19
Chapter Four	Scary Night	23
Chapter Five	Seal Incident	25
Chapter Six	Bad Debts	27
Chapter Seven	Springtime	30
Chapter Eight	Equine Fiasco	34
Chapter Nine	Cricket Debut	36
Chapter Ten	Service Duty	39
Chapter Eleven	War Memories	41
Chapter Twelve	Four Brothers	42
Chapter Thirteen	Holiday Accident	44
Chapter Fourteen	The Beginning	46
Chapter Fifteen	Ayr Academy	50
Chapter Sixteen	Growing Up	53
Chapter Seventeen	Hogmanay	55
Chapter Eighteen	Dodgy Behaviour	60
Chapter Nineteen	Cornwall Continued	62
Chapter Twenty	Happier Days	65
Chapter Twenty-One	Changing Times	68
Chapter Twenty-Two	Glasgow University	73
Chapter Twenty-Three	Stourport on Severn	75
Chapter Twenty-Four	Rickmansworth	91
Chapter Twenty-Five	Stately Home	97
Chapter Twenty-Six	Canada	104
Chapter Twenty-Seven	Yeovil	108
Chapter Twenty-Eight	Charlotte	110
Chapter Twenty-Nine	What's the Time?	112
Chapter Thirty	My Practice	126
Chapter Thirty-One	Sad Times	130
Chapter Thirty-Two	Hypocrite	135
Chapter Thirty-Three	Unusual Incidents	142
Chapter Thirty-Four	Holidays	144
Chapter Thirty-Five	Sherborne	148
Chapter Thirty-Six	Foreign Bodies	153
Chapter Thirty-Seven	Strange Cases	155
Chapter Thirty-Eight	Happy Reflections	170

Chapter One
Cornwall

In September 1965, I set off on a journey for a job interview by train to London, and then I took a short flight to Exeter. The small two-engine aircraft took off twice and very quickly landed again. The pilot told us that a warning light had come on each time. After a visit from flight engineers to the cockpit, off we went for the third time.

This time we got further, and the pilot told us the light had come on again. He said that he would ignore it, which was very reassuring for the passengers. On landing at Exeter, I continued my journey by train, still attempting to recover from the trauma of my first flight since my trip to Canada two years before. So far, three aerial journeys have involved five take-offs!

The train slowly carried me deeper into the West Country, and my great apprehension increased. As a veterinary graduate of the class of 65, I was on my way for an interview as an assistant in a country practice.

The pleasant countryside rolled past, cheering me up, and I cast my professional eye on the cattle grazing in the fields. Then, as we neared St. Austell, the landscape changed dramatically. The enormous pyramids of the China Clay mines loomed in the sky, giving an appearance similar to the Egyptian ones. Dotted between them, I was astonished to see very green fields full of cows. The grass in places looked like snow and was covered with fine clay particles. The streams were milky white. Soon I would know these mines well and the men who worked there.

Most of my fellow passengers were holidaymakers, and as we neared the resort of Newquay, a frantic scramble began in the racks for bags and suitcases. Excited children fought over buckets and spades, and I was submerged in a happy crowd pouring onto the platform almost before the train had rumbled to a stop. Clutching my suitcase, I approached Geoffrey Harvey as he stood at the barrier, puffing a pipe.

A large hand stretched out to greet me, and I looked into a tanned and handsome face with silver hair topping a large frame of around 15 stone. Geoffrey had played rugby and cricket for Cornwall, and his father and grandfather had been vets in the area, while his great grandfather had been a farrier. These were in the days before the local community recognised vets. He was the most important person in the St. Columb area, ahead of the local doctors, vicars, and schoolmasters.

Dressed in a tweed jacket, corduroy trousers, checked shirt and tie, with large, polished brogues, he looked every bit the country vet, and my skinny ten stones made a poor comparison. Wrenching a suitcase from my hand, he beamed "Welcome to Cornwall," as we struggled through the crowds to a battered-looking Ford Consul. It was plastered lavishly in dried mud. I found room for my luggage with difficulty beside an erratic jumble of bottles, clothes, ropes, and general veterinary equipment cascading over the seats. His head seemed almost to touch the roof of the car as he eased his large frame behind the wheel, and we slowly picked our way through the Newquay holiday traffic.

He pointed to a building in the main street, saying, "We have a surgery there twice a week for dogs and cats". Finally, we arrived in St. Columb Major, a charming village near Newquay.

He showed me round the practice premises beside his large and lovely old house named Penmellyn, though the other vets were not around, as it was by now evening. I had a pleasant meal with Mr Harvey and his wife, whom he called by the not very flattering name "Froggie!"

Their live-in servant lady served a nice dinner, with delicious fresh chicken, potatoes and broad beans from his garden. Over this meal, he explained the nature of the work done, my salary, and rent-free house, with private use of a Ford Anglia. He kindly explained that he was used to employing new graduates and would help me as much as possible when I started. I answered all his questions about myself, and he announced that the post was mine, which I happily accepted.

Two weeks later, I managed the same trip entirely by train to commence the great adventure of my life as a vet, and again Mr Harvey met me at Newquay Station for the short few miles drive to St. Columb. After an early start in the day, this time, I arrived in the afternoon. He told me this was an ideal time to start, as the practice was relatively quiet. The farmers were busy with harvests, and the animals being out of doors and in the sunshine were keeping well.

Farms which I would soon get to know intimately slipped past, and in a short time, we entered the village of St. Columb Major, where the practice was based. Past the church, we turned into a small square, and in the tradition of Glasgow graduates, I noted with interest the position of the Red Lion pub.

The car crunched on the gravel in front of Penmellyn, a large impressive old house, and we parked near an old stone building that had been a former stable block. Dogs were barking, and several cars were parked there. We climbed wooden steps to the upstairs, where previously horse food and equipment would have been stored in past years in the days of Mr Harvey's father and grandfather.

"This is our operating room," he said, pointing to a small room with the door ajar and a wooden table in the middle. We entered a larger room filled with shelves of medicine and equipment, and he introduced me to my future colleagues.

Dixon Gunn was a short Scotsman with a moustache, dark hair and cheery, outgoing nature, and I noticed an Edinburgh tie on his checked shirt. One day he would become President of the British Veterinary Association.

By contrast, Owen Pearce gave a shy smile, and I instantly assumed we would get on well. He was tall, slim with brown hair, boyish features, wearing the obligatory checked shirt, Edinburgh Tie and corduroy trousers.

"Leverton completes the staff," Mr Harvey informed me, nodding in the direction of a middle-aged fellow with a ruddy complexion who was stacking bottles. I soon found out he was a helpful, friendly odd job man who was a caretaker for the practice. His duties were legion, including looking after a few hens and calves in the field behind and polishing his master's boots every night. My excited gaze took in the rows of mysterious bottles on the shelves, and I was more interested in the other end of the room where all the modern drugs and equipment were situated.

Impressive red rubber tubes hung from nails on the long wall, and it was festooned with gags, calving ropes, emasculators, and all manner of cruel-looking instruments.

"Leverton will sort out equipment for you, and your car is below in the garage," said Mr Harvey, and in a moment, he was gone. The mention of my car had caused a shiver of excitement since although I had passed my test aged 18, the only driving I had done was on my Canada trip two years ago.

Owen led me downstairs and opened the doors of an enormous garage and workshop, which seemed to be the home of equipment chaos. Parked in a corner was a white Ford Anglia with a red interior and raked back rear window.   As I stared at 492 WRL, my excitement knew no bounds. Unfortunately, the vehicle was filthy, had four bald tyres, and seemed to have a lot of dents.

"Your predecessor tended to have a lot of accidents," joked Owen, and I wondered if it was anything to do with the four bald tyres. Owen started her up and backed into the yard. With the help of Leverton bringing what he requested and Owen helping me, we filled the boot with cardboard boxes to contain bottles, calving ropes, many potions, overalls, instruments and glass syringes, and needles in little metal tins.

Owen showed me the boot of his Morris Minor, which was immaculately neat, with everything carefully labelled and packed tightly in the boot. "Here is an example of how not to do it," he said with a grin, carefully opening the boot of the Anglia used by Dixon.
Inside there was chaos. Somebody had carelessly thrown a pair of mud-caked boots on top of the jumble of equipment. I vowed that my vehicle would never be like that!

Eventually, "Boss" returned and asked me to follow his car to my new home. The old Anglia started the first time, and I followed the Consul through the main square, then along a bit of a lane opposite the Red Lion, taxing my driving skills to the limit. Finally, we pulled up outside an old

7

pebble-dashed bungalow called "Trevean," with a wild overgrown garden outside. My predecessor had not been a keen gardener! The house would be mine, and it was rent and rate free. I soon learned my Boss owned all the properties his assistants occupied. I was to be at Penmellyn at 8 a.m. the next day.

I furtively inspected my new domain, where my wife Marie would join me in a week. The sparsely furnished house had rugs over wooden floors, and the decoration was in a sorry state. A definite odour of damp grew to a peak in the third and last bedroom at the end of the hall, and I decided to keep that door permanently shut. There was a coal-fired range in the kitchen for cooking and the larder full of decomposing food, which I immediately consigned to the dustbin.

Venturing out into the warm August afternoon, I wandered up to the main street, all of a minute's walk, and passing "Melness" on the corner, where Dixon lived with his wife, Valerie. Opposite his house was a general store. I went in to be greeted by a loud cry of "Afternoon Vitinary!" in a gorgeous Cornish accent from a lady grinning from behind the counter.

"Good grief - how do you know that?" I replied in astonishment.

"You be the new lad in Trevean - news do travel fast in a small place like this. Do 'ee 'ave a wife? If not, I can 'elp thee with shopping. We do 'ave most things fresh!"

I explained Marie should join me in around a week, so Mrs Ellery helped suggest essentials, most of which I would have forgotten, and placed them neatly in a large cardboard box. "I expect Marie be a looker with an 'usband like you!" followed me out of the shop.

Back I strolled to Trevean, planning how I could start to make it habitable. As I sat on the toilet contemplating how well my shopping had gone, I was forced to struggle to the lounge with my trousers round my ankles to fetch my Daily Telegraph, proving that I had not remembered everything.

As Mr Harvey had told me, the broom cupboard contained paint brushes and the largest tin of magnolia paint I had ever seen, so I resolved to get busy as soon as I had had an extensive clean-up.

After some beans on toast (standard student meal), I took a stroll round the village, looking at the quaint grey houses and cottages, and ventured up a side lane to the lovely village church with impressive stained-glass windows and a tidy churchyard. Beyond was the village playing field, with a rickety old pavilion. Unusually for a Scot, I was a keen cricketer. I inspected the square with interest, noting the rather bumpy wicket, pausing for a while to visualise the triumphant innings I would hopefully soon play there.

By now, the sun was setting, and I called into the Red Lion and ordered a pint of St. Austell ale, which, after Scottish beer, tasted very

8

bitter to me. The friendly landlord chatted to me as I decided the local brew was an acquired taste, but I would like it with practice. The day had been long and tiring, and despite the lumpy bed, I was soon slumbering, numbed by my journey and two pints.

I began my career on a sunny August Monday, and at 8 a.m., assembled with Dixon and Owen in the little office at Penmellyn. We sat around a large table in a study, with shelves filled with veterinary books and files spilling untidily in all directions. Above a fireplace were racks of pipes and a large porcelain mug from which protruded the corner of a five-pound note.

Soon Boss Harvey, as he was known, arrived and took up his position at the head of the table where he consulted a large neatly written book showing the day's work. A friendly greeting and Dixon was given a list of farm visits with a conversation about follow-ups and how cases were progressing. Happy with his round, Dixon confidently left the room, and I wished that I also had three years' experience under my belt. Owen engaged in friendly conversation about his duties and also left on his missions of mercy.

My boss beamed at me and said, "I've got one for you, Graham. Mr Jones at Shalimar has many calves that need a follow-up injection for lungworm infection. They are about a year old, so give each ten cc. of Caritrol, and say you will check them in a week."

He handed me a well-worn Ordnance Survey Map covered with Biro marks and arrows indicating the location of farms. Soon I was driving down the leafy narrow Cornish lanes, which I would come to know and love, proud to be on my way to my first case.

Mr Jones had a smallholding, and I soon arrived in a yard full of tumbledown sheds. "Mornin' Mister," came a cheery greeting, though his assistant seemed to eye me with suspicion. "You be the new Vitinary?" he inquired. "Fresh outa' college? Gotta start larnin proper now then!" My precarious confidence shook visibly under this starting blow. Nevertheless, I donned my wellington boots, and with my stethoscope, bottles and syringes in my hands, I followed them to a small barn where about twenty steers and heifers aged about a year were coughing and rampaging around.

Some gates were brought and secured, and the frightened animals were driven and jammed behind them. I listened to some chests, and the third heifer lunged suddenly, trapping my fingers painfully in the bars. The helper chuckled at my misfortune as I loaded a syringe and plunged it into the rump of the bullock nearest him. The poor beast kicked out, and a loud crack signified a direct hit on his shin bone. I enjoyed a wry smile to Mr Jones as the helper hopped around cursing.

My mission was accomplished after half an hour of confusion and having my feet trodden on and my waterproof trousers covered in muck.

"Well done, young 'un," said Mr Jones, hosing me down with the yard hose. As I was removing my boots, he thrust two large cauliflowers into my hands. I soon became aware of the habit of giving small gifts as a sign of appreciation and bade him goodbye, receiving a parting grunt from the helper, who held me personally responsible for his bruised shin bone!

Mr Harvey checked on my progress at the office and pointed to my map at Burthy Farm, Summercourt. "A large number of sick pigs with Erysipelas that need penicillin and serum. It should be an easy diagnosis, and then arrange a revisit tomorrow morning."

I found the farm at the end of a winding lane with some difficulty and was greeted by a huge red-faced farmer wearing a cloth cap and resplendent in gaiters. He was pleased to see me and led me quickly into large styes. "They be proper poorly Mister, happen you come just in time. One be gone already!"

One gilt lay dead in the corner, and all the rest were quiet and subdued. Mr Mingo caught another, and I found a high temperature and red diamond-shaped spots on the skin, confirming the suspicions of Mr Harvey. "Erysipelas is a very infectious bacterial disease Mr Mingo, so I suggest we treat every pig which has been in contact, as there is a good chance that serum and antibiotic will save them."

After an hour of pigs screaming in my ears, I was glad to get outside the building. My client was grateful since he knew some neighbours had huge losses with the trouble, and he was happy for me to return the next day. As I cleaned my boots, I accepted his invitation for a cup of coffee in his kitchen.

The smell in the kitchen was only a tiny improvement on the stye, and I regretted my decision. As the kettle boiled on the range, I could not help but notice the unclean condition of the sink. "Good strong coffee," he laughed, holding up a jar of Camp Coffee, a brew that I was not familiar with. The grimy cup made me feel sick, and the drink tasted awful. Finally, he reached for a large tin and prised it open. "Cake?" he asked, and I inspected the mouldy looking sponge cake within.

"No. No, thank you," I managed to reply. Then, swallowing furiously and feigning another urgent call, I exited into the fresh air.

As I leaned out of the Anglia window, I called out to the farmer, "I'll see you tomorrow morning."

"Brilliant job! Perhaps you'll have time for cake tomorrow?"

I felt better on my return to the surgery premises. I spent the rest of the afternoon with Owen making up powders and prescriptions in the top barn. Many of the elderly farmers still liked the older remedies and were suspicious of modern drugs. It was easier often to give both, keep the peace and get the desired result. I enjoyed Owen's amusing quiet company and learned a lot as he tried to encourage me.

That evening I prepared cauliflower cheese for supper and looked forward to Marie's cooking in a week. I had just started to paint the lounge wall when Mr Harvey rang.

"A bad Milk Fever at Arthur at Zealah - she sounds ill, so get there as soon as you can, give one bottle of Calcium intravenously and another subcutaneously."

I knew that Eclampsia in cows who have just given birth was a severe calcium deficiency in the bloodstream, caused by the sudden large amounts going out in milk to the newborn calf, which caused ataxia. The cow would then collapse, with death in a matter of hours. This was my first real emergency, so I whizzed along the lanes and quickly found the village of Zelah. I neared the entrance. I was met by the farmer's wife gesticulating wildly.

"In the field!" she shrieked. "Our best cow!" I fumbled in my car boot for the Calcium bottle, flutter valve and needle box. I ran closely behind her, across the meadow. The cow on her side lay in the corner of the field, with four legs rigid like poles, an hour or less from death.

"Thank God you got here so quickly, Vitinary!" shouted the panic-stricken farmer.

The cow prostate revealed her mammary veins supplying the udder, which was congested with milk, so it was easy for me to insert a sizeable needle into the vein and connect it to the tube to the large bottle of Calcium held high by Mr Arthur. Her calf bellowed beside her as the life-giving mineral dripped into the poor mother's vein.

After about five minutes, the cow was breathing better and managed to sit up, as I gave the second bottle subcutaneously. After another ten minutes came the moment of sheer magic.

I hauled the calf round to her head, and a big knee in the patient's chest resulted in her staggering to her feet and standing unsteadily as the calf shot underneath and started to suckle happily. I gave instructions for the calf to be allowed the colostrum or first milk and then to be reared on artificial milk. This ensured that the amount of milk taken from the mother could be controlled for a while till she fully recovered.

"That sure was a miracle cure Capyn," said the wife, grinning from ear to ear, and my walk back across the field made me feel very content with my performance. Then, as I prepared to climb into the car, the delighted farmer pressed a dozen eggs into my hand. "I know old Harvey gits the money, but you did a proper job, Capyn!"

I was already fond of my new employer, and Owen had told me that two vets were on call each evening and night, and any new assistant was always on call with the Boss. I soon realised that my Boss took all the calls, and I did all the work, but I didn't mind.

Soon the first week had passed, and I excitedly awaited the arrival of my wife at Newquay Station. Amazingly, the train was on time, and my wife

11

Marie (with Scottish pronunciation Maray), fought her way through the holidaymakers and into my arms.

I carried her cases containing the rest of our worldly goods to the white Anglia, which was now very respectable after a clean and polish. "Very smart," observed Marie climbing aboard. "Have you missed me?" she grinned.

"I sure have - I had forgotten what a dreadful cook I am!"

"Is that all?" she laughed as we started back to St. Columb.

"It needs a lot of work," I said, as I carried her over the threshold of our first ever home, "but we'll soon have it shipshape, and I have managed to finish the lounge already," revealing the freshly painted room. After a stroll around the village, we launched a massive clean-up with great youthful enthusiasm as I had the weekend off.

As I was painting in the hall, I heard a crash followed by Marie's scream, and found her in the bedroom at the end of the hall, standing with one foot entirely through the rotten wooden floor which had collapsed. I was so relieved that she seemed unhurt, and we both dissolved into uncontrolled laughter after I helped her out. We closed the door, and I decided I would leave mentioning it to Boss Harvey till an opportune moment arrived.

Gradually the house started to look better, as Marie scrubbed every nook and cranny, cleaned the windows despite my objections about her pregnant state, and I followed with the magnolia paint, the same colour in every room. Later in the day, we drove to Newquay and purchased a few extra furniture pieces from a junk shop.

After half an hour of effort, I stood to admire the kitchen cabinets just acquired and fitted by me on the wall. I was about to start loading plates when they suddenly crashed to the floor. Unfortunately, my university education had not covered the need for rawl plugs!

Despite this minor setback, by Sunday evening, the old place was beginning to look quite acceptable. More visits to Newquay were planned, as we inevitably slowly realised how many items of furniture and everyday things we still needed. After our efforts, we felt delighted on our actual start to our lives together, and we were both soon sound asleep.

Monday morning saw me heading to my first infertility problem at Indian Queens, a village with a strange name. It was supposedly related to a farmer years ago who had brought back a native American bride from the USA.

The tall, wiry old farmer had a great habit of speaking, and somehow at the same time, whistling through his teeth, and I had great difficulty keeping a straight face. I wondered if it was anything to do with his ill-fitting dentures.

"Old Jess (sss) had a dead calf, and now she has whites (sss)", pointing to the white vaginal discharge, which did not smell very healthy. I announced that I would wash the uterus with iodine solution, stripped to the waist, and lathered my arms in soap.

For the first time, my inexperience caught me out as my left arm in the cow's rectum grasped the cervix through the rectal wall, and I attempted with my right arm in the vagina to introduce the catheter into the cervix.

"Is (sss) it in?" Mr Martin enquired, and as I replied that I was not sure, he misheard me and immediately pumped the brown solution as fast as possible. None too confident, I washed myself and equipment and put my shirt back on. Suddenly Jess gave a loud cough, and the brown liquid shot out of the vagina where the catheter must have been.

"By Jove, that worked a lot quicker than when Mr. 'Arvey does (ss) it!" shouted a delighted Mr Martin, and I arranged a repeat visit in a week, which for Jess's sake I would make sure was done by one of my colleagues!

That evening found me on duty, and Mrs (Froggie) Harvey woke me around midnight with a call to see a very ill sheepdog at Trewince farm, which was situated at the end of the runway of St. Mawgan Airfield near Newquay, a Coastal Command base.

A spectacular scene greeted me in the farm kitchen, with a Border Collie in a corner on a blanket and a litter of squeaking puppies a few days old beside her. She was lying rigid on her side, and blood stained the wall behind, where she had bitten her tongue.

The animal had a high temperature, and something shot into my mind from a final year lecture. "I think your dog has Eclampsia, or Milk Fever, the same as you see in your cows," I volunteered.

The astonished farmer replied, "Oi didn't know dogs could 'ave it!"

I trimmed the hair and tied a bandage as a tourniquet around the mother's foreleg before managing to insert a needle into the radial vein, which was not easy with the leg trembling so much. Then, inserting a quantity of calcium intravenously, I followed with a more significant amount subcutaneously in the same way as I had done with a cow a few days before. This would generally have been painful because of the volume. Still, the animal was too near death to feel anything.

A cup of coffee later, and Beth gradually sat up and started to lick her puppies, the rigidity gone from her limbs. "By God, young man, you've done a miracle - she be better already!"

I found some small calcium tablets in my bag as a follow-up treatment and explained that the milk drain was so significant that the puppies (whose father was a Labrador at the next farm) would have to be weaned early. The pair looked doubtful, and his wife volunteered. "We're so busy and have not got time to mess with puppies, but we'll try!"

The thought of the litter dying alarmed me, and though most of the pups were now happily back feeding on Beth, one little black one was crawling

13

from her to where I perched on a chair nearby. "There Vitinary - he does want you to look after 'im! Happen you 'ave a dog?"

"Well, actually no," I hesitated, "but it looks like I do now!" So I reached forward, and a few minutes later, I was on my way back home with a little black object squeaking in my pocket. By now, it was 2 a.m., so I diluted some cow's milk, and used a syringe to feed him, and wondered what on earth Marie would say in the morning?

Little did I think that Tim would witness the birth of my son, see me practice in four English counties, and live long enough to see me start my practice where he remains still buried in the garden.

A week later, the practice was quiet in the afternoon, so Marie and I took an hour off to go to the local Lloyds bank 50 yards from our house. Located in an old stone building in the main street, it looked like a solid, satisfying place, obviously well able to look after my meagre salary. Tentatively, I asked the cashier if it would be possible to open an account. She disappeared and returned to say we were in luck and the manager would see us now. So Marie and I were conducted along a dark corridor to an imposing door with a brass sign reading "R.P. Bennett Manager".

My timorous knock was answered by a loud squeak of "Come in, please!" A small thin, bespectacled man in a dark pin-striped suit leapt from behind his desk as we entered the room. In two bounds, good enough for an Olympic long jumper, he was vigorously shaking our hands and offering us seats before leaping back into his chair. He stared at us as if we had come from outer space. I told him we would like to open a joint account to deposit my monthly salary and have a chequebook. "Excellent!" he cried, fumbling with his Parker fountain pen. "Drink?" he suddenly shouted, so loudly that Marie jumped in her seat. This time Mr Bennett reached a cabinet on the other side of the room in three enormous hops and proudly opened the wooden cabinet, which lit up to display an impressive array of coloured bottles.

"Orange, pineapple, lemonade, grapefruit?" Something told me that asking for a beer was not a good idea, and we settled for two lemonades. Again, he sat in silence before he launched into a tirade about cheque books, life insurance, private pensions and several things about which I knew nothing. We signed a few forms, and as we shook hands to leave, he leapt across the room into the doorway, blocking our way.

"By the way, I am a lay preacher at the Methodist Church, and you would be *most* welcome on Sunday, and we always have tea afterwards! 10.30 a.m. Hope to see you!" he squeaked in farewell, and we exited, trying to control our laughter after his astonishing performance.

Chapter Two
First Winter

As winter approached, the evenings grew darker and colder. The old coal boiler was very unpredictable and frequently went out. I cursed with a box of matches on many freezing mornings, trying to get the coal fire going before boiling a kettle.

No modern amenities those days! Drying clothes often meant operating an old mangle, and Marie struggled to make ends meet on my meagre salary. In a drawer, she kept envelopes marked coal, electric, food etc., in which she saved our insufficient money each week. Nevertheless, we were happy, and on Sundays off duty, we would take Tim down to Watergate Bay and walk along the cliff tops.

As the winter weather grew worse, Marie could no longer come with me due to her pregnancy. I would sometimes don waterproof clothing and a sou' wester to stand on the cliffs on the worst of days, covered in spray, and watching the huge waves crash into the rocks below where the water seemed to boil in anger before rushing back for the next onslaught. How many brave sailors lost their lives navigating the area?

The farms became muddier and muddier, and I wondered how the local farmers managed to cope. So many were more like smallholdings with few large farms and a few modern ones. Some still hand milked a few cows, kept some beef cattle, and often sheep, pigs and hens. The occupants worked long hours, eking out an existence, and if my involvement sometimes ended in the death of an animal, they shrugged their shoulders and thanked me for trying my best.

Many were still suspicious of modern treatments, and woe betides a vet who failed to dispense a coloured drench and say an antibiotic if the patient did not recover.

One farmer, Mr Perkins, a gnarled old fellow in gaiters, cloth cap and a torn old tweed suit, swore by bottles of Blake's Empiric Cattle Remedy. One visit, I arrived a bit early, and he was not around, so I picked up a part used bottle on the shelf of the cow house. I chuckled as I read the different ailments that allegedly could be alleviated, particularly interested in how they could cure constipation *and* diarrhoea!

As he arrived puffing with exertion, I did not realise I was about to participate in an extraordinary incident very early in my career.

"This 'un be beyond me," he grudgingly admitted. "Op on the tractor 'and I'll take 'ee down to her!" On the way, he told me the cow had calved in the morning and was now in a right state. We went through a field full of cattle until we reached a small wood, and a few yards into it was a steep slope with a stream below. She had calved near the wood and was staggering about with Milk Fever. The animal had fallen down the hill into the stream, where she was lying on her side with a helper holding her head above water.

Fortunately, there was plenty of help for once since his neighbours, who I suspected was not too keen on Mr Perkins, were gloating at the apparent dramatic hopelessness of the cow's situation.

I floundered in the stream, water seeping over the top of my wellingtons, and quickly realised that not only did the cow have milk fever, but she had also prolapsed her uterus, which was under water. I told Perkins I could not tell if the fall had broken her back, but I would do what I could.

With plenty of assistants, I managed to give intravenous Calcium into her jugular vein. Still, even if she stood up, I could not see how she would very quickly get out of the stream to where I could deal with the prolapsed uterus since the banks of the stream got worse and higher in each direction.

Perkins shouted that since we had a lot of help, we could put ropes around her and use the tractor to pull her back up the slope. I told him that if she did not already have a broken back, his suggestion risked that happening. Nevertheless, Perkins insisted we try, so I warned him of the dangers, knowing I had plenty of witnesses.

Somehow, we had a considerable supply of ropes and helpers, and I supervised them as they were placed around the patient in several places to distribute the risk. Finally, a few moments later, the ropes were secured to the tractor above the slope, and at my command, we slowly started to pull the cow back up the hill. After a few moments, the poor creature was almost vertical near the top.

"Stop!" I screamed, suddenly having a great idea since the uterus was above the dangling rear end. With gravity 100% on my side, I returned the prolapsed organ with a satisfying plop to inside the cow with fantastic speed, and the tractor slowly resumed the pull till the cow was back on the bank.

The bellowing calf now beside her, and the calcium having taken effect, the cow started to look interested. Then, after five minutes, the farmer's collie came forward near the calf, causing the cow to stagger to her feet in protective mode. I administered an epidural anaesthetic and sutured tape around the vulva to prevent a return of the prolapse and gave some antibiotic cover. However, it occurred to me that the immersion in the stream had given the uterus an excellent clean.

To my amazement, Perkins shouted, "Very well done, lad!" Slowly the cow and calf tottered off into the field, and I enjoyed the congratulations of his neighbours.

As I started back across the field, Perkins assumed I was out of earshot, turned to his neighbours and announced, "Reckon another bottle of Blake's would have done the same thing!"

16

I turned, facing them and shouted, "Next time, Mr Perkins, why don't you try just that."   As I walked on, a red-faced Perkins was suffering deserved ribald abuse from his audience, and I walked off thrilled at an unbelievable result.

Even now, I still recall that day and wonder why the poor cow escaped permanent injury to her back!

I liked Mr Harvey enormously, and he was a marvellous employer for a new graduate. Usually, our cases were picked for simplicity, and I was always well briefed on what to say and do. "Remember, always sound confident," he would say, "and **never** admit you do not know what is wrong with an animal. Then, if all else fails, diagnose the dreaded "Inflammation."

I must admit that I did indeed diagnose quite a few cases of "Inflammation" in my early years.   On farms, this usually brought about solemn nodding from farmers. They were then impressed if the patient recovered after treatment.

Boss Harvey insisted on collar and tie at all times and politeness and respect for the client. One day I put a prescription of intra-mammary tubes of ointment for a cow and labelled it with the address. They were among a pile of medicines awaiting collection sitting in a box outside the entrance of Penmellyn, Boss Harvey's residence.

I was not aware that every morning at 8 a.m., on his way into his study/office to meet us, he had a glance at the medicines awaiting collection by clients.

One morning, he arrived to greet us all in the office, and in his hand was my prescription. "Who prescribed these?" he queried.

"I did, Boss," I admitted.

Looking at the box, he slowly read, "Brewer Lanvean", and shouted, "**Mr Brewer Lanvean** to you!" Then, he threw the box onto my lap and waited till I altered the writing on it.

As we all returned late afternoon from our farm rounds, around five p.m., a few clients would arrive with dogs and cats, hoping that they would be seen, usually by whichever vet was around and nearest.

One evening as I exited my car, I noticed a lady waiting with a Jack Russell in her arms ahead of me. I knew that some gipsies had caravans and ponies tied on a piece of common land just outside the village, and from her unkempt appearance, I suspected that was from where she came. Unusually Mr Harvey was coming down the rickety steps, and the lady asked him to look at the dog. "Would you like to step up to the consulting room, Madam," he replied, doffing his cloth cap and following her upstairs. I had learned another lesson in etiquette!

The only facet of his character I was not so keen on was his meanness. Each day at the end of our rounds, we cleaned our glass syringes of various sizes and placed them with the different sized stainless-steel needles into a large metal box. Then, they were to be put into boiling water on a calor gas ring and sterilised for reuse in the morning.

Every week or so, the assistants would gather in a huddle to nominate a spokesperson in the Oliver Twist tradition, to ask Boss for some new needles to replace blunt ones. Usually, he pointed to a file nearby and told us to use it on the tips. Similar enquiries about unsafe car tyres would result in him kicking them and mumbling, "O.K. for a bit yet!"

The lack of tread on my tyres soon nearly cost me injury on a wet Saturday evening as I headed to an urgent calving case near Newquay. Turning off the main road into the narrow bends with high hedges and blind corners, I wondered what the problem over the calving would be when I came round a corner and saw another car ahead on the narrow lane.

I stood on the brakes and skidded for what seemed an age before hitting the stationary Austin Cambridge head-on with a tremendous bang. Then, very shaken with bruised knees, I emerged to find an elderly gentleman staring at his mangled bonnet, where steam was rising from his damaged radiator. The front of my Anglia was in a similar state.

He proceeded to tell me that he had bought the car new and cleaned it weekly for three years, and it was his pride and joy. He was incensed by my dangerous driving and wanted to call the police. This was not helped by Tim, who had got out of the Anglia and was cocking his leg on the back wheels of the Austin!

I explained the reason for my haste, which failed to appease him, and gave all my details. Fortunately, another motorist had arrived by this time, done a U-turn in a gateway to a field, and offered to take the gentleman home first and myself back to St. Columb.

Thankfully, the victim of my driving had calmed down a bit. After dropping him off at Newquay, the helpful motorist took me back to the surgery, where Dixon called Owen to go to the calving by another route and rang the practice garage to sort out the site of my catastrophe. Dixon kindly offered to tell Boss Harvey, and Tim and I walked home to little sympathy from Marie.

Chapter Three
My Trial

Boss Harvey telephoned and asked me to attend his office at eight p.m. to be interviewed by the police. I duly arrived feeling very apprehensive. Boss was not very happy, and the Sergeant in charge of the small local set-up arrived. "Come in, Tom!" invited Mr Harvey, sounding pleased to see him. "Quick sherry with me?"

"I shouldn't, Sir - not on duty."

"No one will know," answered Mr Harvey, pouring two large glasses of Harvey's Cream from a bottle that had mysteriously appeared in the room. "How are Marge and the boys?" and an earnest discussion followed on their lad's future and employment prospects, with Boss offering recommendations to some local employers.

Mr Harvey kept dominating the general conversation while refilling the glasses again, not including me. Eventually, he turned to me, saying, "This silly bump that my assistant had will, of course, result in my insurance repairing the damage to the other car. I am sure he will drive carefully in future after the jolly good rollicking I have given him."

"Well," began the sergeant, "it's not so simple, Sir. It could be called dangerous driving."

"I've known you for a long time, Tom, and I'm sure you can deal with it in your efficient way with a severe warning," said my boss hopefully, refilling his glass again. Then, after a long pause, Tom turned to me and warned me in no uncertain terms in a booming voice that another further transgression in my car would be dealt with very severely, making it sound like a death sentence was not out of the question! He then sat down again, pleased with his performance and the pleasant conversation was resumed.

I had learned yet another lesson. Eventually, after much handshaking between them, he tottered off swaying slightly.

After Boss had seen him out, he said firmly, "I won't do that a second time!"

To my surprise, he asked me to come into the lounge beside the fire, produced another two glasses and a bottle of whisky, and we spent a social hour as he told me he was pleased with my efforts so far and hoped I was enjoying the practice.

He then talked about the past, and as I stared at the flickering embers, I could imagine his father leaving the fire on a cold night to drive off in an old car, or indeed his grandfather riding off on his horse after a farmer had called at the door in days before telephones. He explained how his grandfather would have been sleeping and hoping for a quiet night in the night-time of many years ago.

In days gone by, the practice was a solo one and would not cover the distances now covered by the car. To hear the clattering of hooves coming up the hill where the house was usually meant an urgent call. If the noise continued into the village centre, it meant it was the local doctor's turn to vacate his warm bed!   In the days of horse travel, his grandfather worked on his own and distances were limited to where a horse could travel reasonably.

Even now, in 1965, many farm clients had never been as far as Exeter. The old lady who delivered my newspaper had been to St. Columb Road as a small child to see the railway that had just reached Newquay many years ago.   It was rumoured that the three miles in a cart was her furthest lifetime journey.   To her, Exeter was no different to Tokyo or Alice Springs.

One of the areas that fascinated me was the St. Austell clay mines, only a few miles distant. The white pyramids of upturned clay varied in appearance all the year-round, and with a red sunset behind, had an almost Egyptian appearance. In between were small fields, and the cattle there were owned by exceptional families. Miners rented the small fields behind them. They had started with a couple of animals raised for beef, and gradually they progressed, hoping for the day they could rent enough areas to sustain a living without the mine.

Most would rise before dawn, milk some cows, go to work in the pits, come home, milk cows again, do work in the fields, then collapse in bed before the next day! Seven days a week! If they prospered, they bought a few more animals, always dreaming of the day they could give up their job in the mines and become a full-time farmer.

Their dedication and hard labour amazed me, and quite how the cows grazed without suffering any mineral poisonings or difficulties astounded me, and they did not even blink when dynamite was routinely exploded in the pits around. I well remember my own first experience giving me quite a scare.

One miner who had made it as a full-time farmer was Mr Jacobs, and one day I was asked to attend to give a cow a sedative.   Arriving at the smallholding, he was not around for once, and I found a single cow tied in a stall in deep straw. Waiting for someone to appear, I noticed how fragile she was, with sores on her hocks, a shrivelled udder, and she was munching on a massive pile of cow nuts.

Mrs Jacobs appeared from the house and told me that this was Mabel, the first cow they ever bought - she was at least twenty years old and had not had a calf for ten years! "Poor Joe can't bear to see her go, but now she has difficulty standing up, and he has said goodbye to her. Hargreaves, the knacker man, is coming at noon, and Joe wants you to give her a strong sedative, so the poor beast won't feel being shot! He is indoors sobbing his heart out an' won't come out," she told me.

I gave an enormous dose of sedative to Mabel, and she looked me in the eye without concern, returning happily to her final feast. Finally, I wrote a note for Hargreaves, warning him that the meat must not be used for pet or human consumption. I had visions of steak pies in the local pub sending customers to sleep or the local hounds nodding off permanently! Such was the spirit of these 'miners come farmers', and I would always admire them.

There was little small animal work in the early sixties, and since our experience was limited, it was not unusual for two vets to consult together.

Mr Brewer was a wizened older man with a sheep farm on the moors, and incredibly his young sheepdog was a littermate of my Tim, so I knew at least one more had survived. His name was Sandy though he was black and white!

"I reckon he be poisoned Mister as 'ee 'asnt eaten for four days and do throw up all the time!" Then, as my hands closed over Sandy's slim abdomen, I could palpate a large lump and enquired if he had been given any bones to chew?

"Not that I know of," was the reply.

I volunteered that I thought Sandy had a bowel obstruction and needed an exploratory operation. This diagnosis appeared to greatly please Mr Brewer till he narrowed his eyes and asked timidly, "What does that cost?"

"Let's worry about that later," was my reply after Owen had examined the dog and agreed with my plan.

Mr Brewer left the friendly young dog with us, going off to ponder his account, and we boiled a tray of surgical instruments and homemade drapes. Owen gently gave the intravenous Thiopentone and shaved and cleaned the abdomen. Gingerly I made an incision and lengthened it over the area of the obstruction, finding part of the small intestine distended and vivid red with inflammation of the site. I penetrated the intestine, and the stench of contents filled the air as I removed the obstruction in one piece.

"It's binder twine!" cried Owen as I dropped the mess in a stainless-steel tray. I cleaned the site and slowly sutured the bowel, sprinkled the area with Sulphanilamide powder, checked the remaining bowel for any other abnormalities, and closed the wound, as Owen removed the needle from the vein.

Owen gave a hefty dose of antibiotic, and we wrapped Sandy in a blanket with a hot water bottle (no intravenous fluids available at the time) and placed him on straw in a kennel in the barn.

The next day, being young and robust, Sandy was like a new dog and was given a small drink of milk which stayed down.

At that time, binder twine was ubiquitous on farms. The young pup had been playing with some of it, which had tangled in his mouth, and the easiest way out was to swallow it!

Later that day, a delighted Mr Brewer left with instructions to give lots of little drinks and small meals for a week.

A week later, Sandy came bounding in for his sutures to be removed, and a pleased owner left, knowing he still had a future working dog from a trained mother.   He was still panicking about his bill, which was up to Mr Harvey and not us.   Owen and I were proud of the happy result.

Chapter Four
Scary Night

Night calls were a common occurrence from farmers, and at 2 a.m. I picked up the telephone to Boss Harvey's disembodied voice as my brain struggled to function. "I have a calving for you," was the message, and he gave me details of the village which was not easy to find, and he told me what to expect.

"The farmer lives with his three sons, and they are all dwarfs - don't be alarmed, they are accommodating, so make sure you give each a job! There is no electricity on the farm, but old Roper will be grateful, and you will get a whisky afterwards in the ingle with his tall tales while you warm up!"

Armed with this extraordinary information, I found the lane which led to the place, and at the gate was a figure with a massive white beard swinging an oil lamp. Scurrying around him were three shadowy figures less than half his size. With a dog barking behind, complete with a full moon, it gave a scenario like arriving at Dracula's Castle, and I emerged from the car with great trepidation.

"Thanks for comin' Vitinary. My lads have soap and water ready for 'ee!"

Two oil lanterns lighted the cowshed, and a giant South Devon cow stood there with a single leg protruding from the rear end. Even in those days, the breed was rare, which I regarded with sadness, as I already had a soft spot for these amiable giants.

Two of the sons quarrelled over the soap and bucket, but I remembered my instructions from Boss. So I put one in charge of the bucket and soap, one with the large towel, and one to help his father hold the cow still. This action seemed to solve the situation immediately, and their father stood by the cow's head, puffing an old pipe.

Finding the calf coming backwards, I tried to locate the other hind leg. But, hard as I wanted to bring it into position, the powerful contractions of the mother were working against me and hurting my arm, which was being squeezed against the pelvic bone. "I shall have to give her an Epidural," I announced, washing my hands and asking for my bag. A delighted small person leapt from the shadows, and with scissors, I clipped the golden curls over the base of the spine. Then, carefully feeling the area, I found the correct spot between the vertebrae and inserted a long needle enabling me to inject a local anaesthetic into the spinal canal. I then showed the owner how the cow's tail was now limp. Next, I reinserted my arm into the uterus, and with no contractions, it was pretty simple for me to bring the other back leg out.

The sons leapt forward with my calving ropes, and after much lubrication was applied, I arranged the three boys on one rope while I took the other. Finally, after some organised traction, the calf gradually appeared. "Now! One last big pull!" I shouted, and a large slimy, steaming calf tumbled into the straw. Quickly I checked there was not another calf, something my boss had told me never to forget.

I leapt on the calf, clearing its mouth, and vigorously rubbing its chest with straw. The farmer untied the cow, and she immediately turned round to start licking her offspring.

By the time I had washed up, dried, and replaced my shirt, the calf was standing up, to the delight of the boys who buzzed around me excitedly.

"Well done, Mister, come into the house, and I'll get 'ee a drink."

I followed him into the farmhouse, lit by lanterns, and he directed me to the enormous ingle where I could sit by a log fire. Warming my hands on the flames, I stared up the long chimney and thought I could glimpse the stars.

As the young lads flitted in the shadows, he handed me an enormous whisky and sat down drinking another. "My wife died 'avin' the last boy, so it be just the four of us now and the cattle," he said. He then told me that he was working on board a tea clipper ship when he was my age and regaled me with scary tales of going round the Cape of Good Hope in a gale. "What seas! Waves the size of this house!" I was happy Boss Harvey had forewarned me, and I was fascinated by the whole surreal night.

Assisting animals into the world always gave me great satisfaction, and I was always astonished at how quickly independent they became. Lambing time in the spring was great fun, and I quickly became an expert at sorting out all manner of combinations of heads and limbs tangled in all varieties of twins and sometimes triplets. My small hands were an advantage, and soon farmers were even asking me to attend if possible. For example, in comparison, Boss Harvey had hands like shovels compared to mine. Throw in the occasional caesarean section, and I was happy every spring lambing time, which I still consider the happiest days of farm work.

Chapter Five
Seal Incident

One wild afternoon a call came through from the Newquay R.S.P.C.A., requesting help with an injured seal.   Since that afternoon was quiet, somebody suggested that Owen and I go together and take a large net from the barn.

We met the R.S.P.C.A. Inspector at the new lifeboat station site under construction near Padstow, where the slipway would lead down into the water from the cliff.   The place was busy with all manner of lorries, temporary huts, and building equipment everywhere.

Inspector Hale, a rotund cheery soul, extended his hand to us. "I think it is a young one, stranded on the beach, but with all the rocks around, it could be injured; besides, I'm a bit old to go down there." The last part of his advice caused Owen and I to exchange a worried look.

The foreman attired us in coats and hard hats and took my case and the net. We followed him into a shed on the cliff edge and started down a makeshift staircase, going past metal girders pinned to the cliff face.

Climbing onto another set of steps with less protection on the sides, through gaps in the structure, I could see the sea crashing onto the rocks and beach below while rain lashed us and the wind howled. The next level seemed as far as the girders had progressed, and an ominous trapdoor lay at one end.

The foreman asked us to follow him and grabbed a rope ladder which descended about 40 feet onto a piece of sand among the rocks. As he started down one at a time, the ladder swung from side to side in the howling wind. "Throw your bag and net down, and I will try to hold the ladder still, as the seal is close by!"

"I can't do it!" I shouted, but my cries could not be heard over the wind. A burly workman was already lifting me through the hole, where I grabbed the rope ladder and swung about till I managed to get my feet on it lower down. I descended slowly, sick with fright, clinging to the slimy rope with my eyes shut. Then, as I had a quick peep, I could see the cliff come close, then move away as the rope swayed with the foreman on the lower end, trying hard to control it.

My knuckles were white as I made slow progress imagining my fate on the rocks if I passed out. Finally reaching the safety of a small piece of sand, my legs buckled, and I toppled onto the beach flat on my back. Rain dripped down my collar, and the deluge lashed my frozen face. As I regained my composure, an ashen-faced Owen joined me.
The foreman chuckled and told us that a walk along the beach would lead to a hill climb back to the road on the way back.

Feeling much better after this advice, we found the baby seal a short way away, and it hissed menacingly at us. Quickly we caught it in the net, and I grabbed its tail, lifting it off the ground.

25

Owen sprayed a cut on its back with an antibiotic aerosol, and it seemed so strong that we deduced that it had been washed ashore, somehow been disorientated, and turned away from the sea. We dragged it back into the sea and got wet, releasing it in the water, aware that all this time its anxious mother was a few yards away, popping her head above the water to keep us in view.

With wet lower halves, we started down the beach, and as we looked back, we could eventually witness a happy family reunited, which made us immensely proud.   Half an hour later, we made it up the hill and walked back along the road, wishing we had come that way in the first place. The workers thanked us and were greatly amused when I observed that whatever they were paid, it should be doubled.

Chapter Six
Bad Debts

One of the biggest problems for Mr Harvey was collecting his fees from clients, mainly farmers not keen to part with their money. We could never refuse to see a sick animal, and clients would take advantage of this.

One of the worst was Mr Reed, who always owed a significant amount. Every Friday was the local cattle market, and Boss Harvey frequently listened to gossip and, more importantly, corner clients and quietly suggested they do something about their accounts.
Mr Harvey noticed Mr Reed in the crowd and gradually managed to get closer and closer to him.

Mr Reed had realised the situation and tried to keep his distance, finally walking smartly off and disappearing into the car park where he started his ancient Hillman Minx. Mr Harvey had arrived at the exit to the main Newquay Road and was waiting for him. Mr Reed deliberately looked the other way before entering the road to avoid eye contact, and this proved to be his downfall, as he crunched into, of all things, a police car returning to Newquay.

The two officers in the car were astonished to find that Mr Reed had not only no road tax or insurance but had never held or attempted to hold a driving licence. Despite this, he had driven weekly to market for the last forty years and would probably have got away with it indefinitely had he paid Mr Harvey's bill!

As Christmas approached, Marie expanded in size, and her mother Jean arrived from Scotland to help her run the house in the latter days of her confinement. This was not a problem since I liked and got on well with my mother-in-law. I was relieved that Marie had company when I was at work, especially evenings and night calls. However, two days before her due date, I had to take her to the local doctor with a bout of diarrhoea.

The following day the weather was atrocious, with driving rain and howling winds rocking the foundations of our little bungalow. Marie spent all evening visiting the toilet complaining of severe constipation, so I telephoned the doctor for advice.

He listened carefully, reassured me that all was well, and checked that I had the correct number for the local midwife if anything seemed to happen. I discovered afterwards that he had just gone to bed, and his wife, already a friend of Marie, asked about the call she had overheard.

"You told me Marie had diarrhoea yesterday? You silly fool, she'll have that baby by the morning!"

Suitably reassured, I returned to find Marie pacing up and down complaining of abdominal pains. As she wandered back and forth in the house, Tim followed her, wagging his tail, wondering if the commotion meant a walk was imminent. To add to the absurd situation, a voice kept

27

coming from the guest bedroom, as mother-in-law continually enquired, "Is it false labour?"

Whatever false labour was, I had had enough and rang Miss Pothecary, the midwife.

She agreed to attend as soon as possible, but since she lived alone in a village on the coast, and there was a howling gale, she might be some time. I managed to get Marie into bed, as the foetal membranes had just ruptured, and her contractions were steadily increasing. Calls of enquiry were still coming from the guest room, and I shouted in exasperation, "It's **NOT** false labour. I can see the baby's head!" At that very moment, I heard a car pull into the drive, not a moment too soon.

The wind nearly pulled the door off its hinges, as Miss Pothecary, all six feet of her (I had not met her before at Marie's check-ups), burst into the house, like the cavalry in a John Wayne film. I already had hot water, towels etc., ready, finding it amusing that the tables were turned on in my usual situation.

"Hammer a nail in the wall, in case we need a drip," she said.

This sentence did little to reassure Marie, as Miss Pothecary went about organising Marie's efforts in a very dominating manner. "Come on, girl, it's not that painful," shouted Miss Pothecary, eliciting the reply, "How do you f------- well know! You've never done this!" The only time I ever heard Marie use a swear word.

Within a short period, my son and heir was bawling lustily and wrapped in a warm blanket, and everything went smoothly. Tim, who until then had kept out of the way, was seen creeping out of the room with a rolled-up newspaper containing the afterbirth. He was rather partial to eating those of cows I had calved on farms and was displeased that I considered this a different situation, as I snatched his prize away when I finally caught him in the garden.

Mother-in-law had by now appeared in dressing gown and curlers and made tea for the happy little party as dawn broke to greet the new arrival. I thanked Miss Pothecary, whom I knew had delivered most of the local babies for many years and must have had to cope with many serious situations with the nearest hospital at Newquay.

A couple of hours later, my new family safely arrived, and it was off on a morning round.

I felt ten feet tall, and at lunchtime, I went to the village chemist shop, obeying instructions.

Nick the chemist, already a friend, saw me in the shop and rushed out with congratulations, proving the bush telegraph had been operating again.

I then asked his assistant for a supply of nappies and pins. "Which kind would you like?" was the reply, and I said, "Any kind will do," desperate to be home as soon as possible.

As mother-in-law opened the pharmacist's bag, my offspring was already tucking into breakfast (more than I had managed). "Look what you've got! Pink pins!" she cried, and Marie laughed as John started life in pink nappy pins.

As the months rolled by, springtime came, the weather improved, and the leafy banks returned to the Cornish lanes.

Chapter Seven
Springtime

I was fortunate to live in such a beautiful part of Southwestern England, and spring was a lovely time of year before the main arrival of the tourists. When possible, I sometimes attended the charming village church in the village centre, and John Graham Tremayne was duly christened in the quaint old structure as the sun shone through the windows.

However, this was not without a blip, caused by Canon Cook's memory, when after being told the child's name, christened him "John Graham Tre... What did you say?"

The local vicar Canon Cook was quite a character, with a mop of white hair and a reputation for a short memory. Occasionally he failed to show up for weddings or funerals, sending panic-stricken searchers to the vicarage close by, where he would be found mowing his lawn or asleep in his deckchair in the garden, after a gin and tonic!

Many years later, in the late seventies, I was on holiday with my family at a caravan park near Newquay, and I had a puncture in my beloved black Rover SDI. Having changed the wheel, I drove the few miles to the garage in St. Columb Major, which Mr Harvey's practice had used.

In my day, Jack Teagle, a friend of mine, owned it, and I found he was now sadly deceased, but his son still ran it, who had been a young lad then. I was astonished when he recognised me and called me by name, and he agreed to replace the tyre while I waited. An old Morris 1000 arrived outside, and the elderly driver got out of the car as we arranged this.

"You will recognise this customer," said my friend, and I then immediately saw an older version of Canon Cook approaching. "Sorry to not phone up, but I wonder if you would have time to check my brakes, please?" he enquired.

Young Teagle asked the vicar to leave the keys in the car, and he would look at it as soon as possible and telephone to discuss the problem.

"Thank you so much!" The vicar exclaimed, left the office, went back to his car and drove off. Mr Teagle turned to his apprentice and asked him to walk downtown to the vicarage and fetch the car.

"You can see that Canon Cook still has the same memory," said the owner as we laughed away together.

One day I was asked to examine an eight-year-old male Corgi, who presented with virtually no hair on his body. This baldness had happened over a month, and he had no irritation as a result. However, on examination, I found only one testicle present and a huge mass in the abdomen. I told the owners that I suspected a nasty tumour called a Sertoli Cell tumour, and the growth was undoubtedly in an abdominally retained testicle.

That day I opened the abdomen and removed the tumour, which was the size of a small football. Then, I removed the other testicle simultaneously, reasonably confident of the outcome.

The owners were amazed when the dog redeveloped a nice coat within a month and had a new lease of life.

I wrote the case up and sent it to the Veterinary Record, the animal equivalent of the Medical Lancet, and was amazed when they printed it. From the U.S.A. to even a Soviet Union University, I received many requests for reprints of the article. Unfortunately, this proved to be expensive in postage costs!

Many years later, I performed the same operation on a Beagle belonging to a young lad I knew, working as a bricklayer. As well as removing the Sertoli Cell tumour and the normal testicle, I found in the abdomen a complete uterus and two vestigial ovaries, which I also removed. The dog made a full recovery and was a genuine hermaphrodite. When Wayne told his mates on the building site, he was subject to many ribald comments for some time.

Most farms had been in generations of Cornish men, and one exception was a farm recently purchased by an unmarried retired Army Officer, who decided to retire to Cornwall and live in a small farm.

I once read, "Never go into a business you know nothing about," and Colonel Barkworth proved the point, struggling with a small herd of North Devon beef cattle, helped by an elderly worker who did everything. Unfortunately, however, the helper was not around when I arrived, answering a call to calving at 2 a.m.

As I arrived sleepily in his yard, he greeted me with cheery efficiency. "Here we are, old boy, hot water, soap, and a towel, all ready for you!"

Noting the neat arrangement of the equipment, I enquired where the patient was.

"She's over in the far-field," was the reply.

"In the field?" I retorted somewhat incredulously. "How are we going to catch her?"

He replied that the cow was lying down.

"She may be lying down now, but I doubt if she is when we approach. I think you had better find a rope halter," I replied, sensing imminent disaster.

The night was pretty dark, with little moonlight, and we set off, the Colonel
carrying my bag, ropes and halter, while I took the bucket of water, soap, and towel. We descended into a copse through a rough field, with a steep climb out of the other side. Although dry, the ground we crossed was soaked by several days of rain, and we slipped and slithered on the tricky slope. With every stumble on the rough ground, I had lost more of the water, and the soap had vanished.

Eventually, I surveyed the herd, illuminated now quite well by the moon, which had suddenly emerged from behind the clouds. The North Devon cows stared and eyed me with that incredible curious and disinterested look that only a bovine possesses. They continued to chew the cud, as if to say, indifferently, "Yes, I've seen you, but you don't look particularly interesting, so I'll just keep tucking into my grass."

The Colonel puffed away behind me, and I reflected that his career must have ended behind a desk. "Over there, old boy!" he said, pointing to a sick looking cow, lying with her ears down.

"Try to get the halter on her head!" I shouted as my patient struggled to her feet and tottered away faster than the Colonel could run. I could see a swollen head of a calf protruding from her rear end, with a grossly swollen blue tongue sticking out, showing it had been dead for some time. "Our only hope is to try to chase her into the corner by the gate!" I called without thinking we had much chance. As we pursued her, I could hear the Colonel's breathing sound more and more distressed, and his face got very red, making me wonder whether I might end up having to treat him!

As we neared the gate, the field became muddier still, ending near the entrance in a veritable quagmire, and my wellington boots threatened to part from my feet. As she reached the gate, the cow finally collapsed in the mud, unable to move.

We got the halter on her head, and the portly Colonel sat on her back, still puffing heavily. The area was a mass of glutinous mud, reminiscent of the battlefields of Passchendaele.

My bag was covered in mud, and most of the water in the bucket had been lost in the pantomime. Since the calf was long dead and hugely swollen, I decided that desperate measures were required. I found a fret saw and scalpel in my bag, and after much crude sawing and cutting, I managed to remove the dead calf's head.

Using the remains of the water and all the cotton wool I had in my bag, I attempted to clean the area around the vulva before removing my shirt. Then, reaching into the uterus, I located both front legs, exteriorised them, and placed my calving ropes around them; I pulled with all my might, trying to coincide with the mother's contractions. But, unfortunately, with one final effort, it resulted in the headless dead calf and vet being hurtled backwards to fall in the mud.

Covered in mud and blood, I must have been a pretty picture with a headless body in my lap. First, I attempted to clean my hands as much as possible by rubbing them on any dry hair on the cow. Next, I injected a massive dose of antibiotics into the animal, along with some similar uterine pessaries.

I explained to the Colonel that there was a severe risk that the cow would die of septicaemia from the prolonged labour and not too sterile delivery, but there was no other option. So we climbed through the gate, and to our amazement, the cow managed after a struggle to get back on

32

her feet. She re-joined her mates who by now were all around us, fascinated by the performance. I shivered on the return trip to the farmhouse, with the Colonel puffing behind carrying my clothes.

As we entered the kitchen, he prodded the embers of a log fire and disappeared upstairs to run a bath. Discarding my muddy clothes, I climbed in and washed mud and blood from my hair and upper body, but felt instantly better, even though my shirt was none too clean to reuse, but at least my trousers were dry after I removed my over trousers at the back door. It reminded me of the large bath we piled into in my school rugby playing days.

I came downstairs to a delicious smell of bacon cooking, the fire had recovered, and the Colonel thrust a large whisky into my hand. He was delighted that the cow now had a chance of surviving, and we enjoyed an early breakfast as he regaled me about trying to fry eggs and bacon on his hot tank at El Alamein during the war. Amazingly the cow recovered and had calves for years afterwards, and the Colonel often asked for me when he needed any visits made. So I was pretty proud of that incredible night.

I always marvelled at the immune system of cattle, who seemed to survive situations that other species did not.

As a veterinary surgeon, I was expected to be familiar with a wide range of species, and at the time of my student days, the horse, though declining in importance, was still worthy of many studies. However, converting my knowledge into practical success mostly eluded me. Many horse owners were overbearing and opinionated, difficult to please, and I did not enjoy their company too much at times.

I remember talking to a retired vet who had served in the Veterinary Corps in the Great War. These days, all horses are vaccinated against "Glanders", an infectious disease, with an injection into the eyelid, and he described a morning vaccinating a hundred at a time.

How did you get them to hold still?   It seemed to be a reasonable question. He replied all vets started as Captains, and many soldiers had worked with horses or on farms. So all he had to do was order as many privates as needed to hold down any wild horse. This was achieved easily by the sheer weight of numbers, meaning the poor horse could not move a muscle.

Chapter Eight
Equine Fiasco

This was not the case when I visited Miss Phillips large bay hunter with a gash on his back leg. "If there is no more help, could you please hold up a front leg?" I asked her hopefully.

"Jolly good, fire away!" came the reply.

I approached the horse's rear end with a syringe full of local anaesthetic and, grasping the leg with my left hand, gently pushed in the needle with my right. The patient leapt in the air, lashing out and just missing me with its hind legs. Then, a split second later, I was on my back and covered in the broken glass of my syringe.

"Sorry about that! Too strong for me!" bellowed Miss Phillips, shouting obscenities at the shivering horse, which made him worse but seemed to help her.

Since we were in a loose box with deep straw, and no more help was available, I made a suggestion. "We have a new sedative drug which will hopefully make him very sleepy?" I volunteered.

"Top hole! Have a bash with it," was her immediate reply.

Not having used the drug before, I carefully computed the dose, and after Miss Phillips got hold of a bridle, I managed to plunge the medicine into the hunter's neck muscle. "Now walk him round the room, as it takes a while to take effect," said I, trying to sound confident.

Gradually the horse began to puff and sweat, and his legs began to wobble. Then, appearing to fight the drug's effect, he began to travel faster and faster on his circuits, with Miss Philips struggling to hang on. Unfortunately, as the horse's speed increased, my position by the door became more hazardous with every course. Finally, I shot out of the door to my shame, listening horrified to loud bangs and oaths from Miss Phillips.

Finally came a crash and silence, and I peered in to see the horse on his side and a red-faced, puffing owner sitting on top of him. "Jolly exciting," she observed as I took note of an extra couple of new wounds on the horse, while thankfully, the owner was unhurt.

I quickly popped the local in, sutured the wounds in record time, gave a tetanus injection, and suggested some blankets round the side of the box, a good idea, as the horse slowly sat up looking puzzled. Miss Phillips was delighted, and to my horror, suggested that next time she had a similar problem, she would specifically ask for me to come!

Fortunately, not all horses were the same, and I remember treating Jack, an enormous elderly Shire with a hoof abscess. Every day for a week, I called in, asked him to lift his poorly leg, which he placed onto my lap while I cut away a bit more hoof and cleaned the pus. It must have hurt, but every day he dutifully lifted the leg on request. Perhaps he realised that I was four years younger than him and decided to be kind to the youngster.

Chapter Nine
Cricket Debut

Spring was turning into summer when I went to buy some garden tools in the ironmongers in the main street of St. Columb. A young assistant came to help and seemed to know who I was. "I'm Geoff, captain of the St. Columb Cricket team, and I heard that you played cricket?"

I was off duty that Saturday, and within minutes, he talked to me about turning out for the local team. After a long chat and purchasing garden tools at "cricketer's discount" rates, I wandered home speculating how Marie would feel about my plans.

"I wondered how long it would be until I had to look out and clean your kit!" she laughed, bowing to the inevitable. The rest of the week saw me cleaning my bat and whitening my boots while dreaming of illustrious deeds on Saturday.

"We meet at the Ring of Bells at 1 p.m., so must be away at St. Dennis, so I have no idea when I will be back," I volunteered, kissing Marie and John in her arms at the door.

The Ring of Bells, perched on the hill into St. Columb near Boss Harvey's practice, was busy, and the small bar was packed with cricket equipment untidily shoved in a corner.
Geoff cried out in delight and soon introduced me to my teammates whilst he acquired a pint of St. Austell Ale for me.

The team consisted of farmers, villagers, and three service members from St. Mawgan R.A.F base nearby, including the camp doctor, who in time became a good friend. So naturally, the noise level increased as we graduated to the third pint with much hilarity. Slightly alarmed about the journey length to St. Dennis, I asked Geoff how long it would take and was shocked to discover that we were playing at home for the first time!

"We're leaving after this drink," said Geoff.

Soon we emerged from the dark little bar into the bright sunlight of the June afternoon, and the team slowly walked the 50 yards past the church to the cricket field, where the opposition was already practising outside the old green wooden pavilion.

Friendly greetings were exchanged, and I glanced at the white-clad enemy, who ranged from tall teenagers to grey-haired gentlemen, with portly tummies held in by coloured ties round their flannels.

On the way, I had noticed the somewhat uneven looking wicket, with a local teenager still painting white lines near it. They did not seem too straight, and I wondered if he had also been in the Ring of Bells.

We quickly changed in the rickety old pavilion, and as Geoff had lost the toss, we went out to the field, applauded by the opposition perched on chairs outside. Geoff sent me to field at midwicket, and I was soon busy. The St. Dennis openers received several short balls, usually hooked around me to the boundary, with several ending in a bed of nettles where I acquired several stings and wondered if all new players had to field in that position?

Soon, one of the St. Mawgan lads came on to bowl first change, with good direction and lively pace, and quickly took three wickets.

The last was a fantastic return catch, where he dived full length hanging on to the ball, and he tumbled over spectacularly, emitting a loud shriek, "Oh no! Not again!" Some sort of panic surrounded the bowler lying flat on his back.

Geoff ran over to me and said, "You had better take a look, Graham!"

I could see Jim's trouser leg covered in blood, and he shouted, "It's out again, and now I'm going to miss the start of the rugby season!" I lifted his trouser leg and was horrified to see the end of a bright stainless-steel plate as it protruded from his shin. By this time, the umpire had fainted, and several fielders looked very pale.

I supported Jim from the field as he moaned about missing his cricket and rugby and learned this was the second time the plate had come out while playing scrum-half for his Air Force team.

All of this time, the camp doctor, who considered himself off duty, was enjoying a crafty cigarette on the boundary! Then, finally, someone ran to a shop to ring an ambulance, and the game resumed.

I bowled my off-breaks and got three wickets, as St. Dennis were dismissed for 149. During tea and sandwiches, Geoff enquired what position I usually batted.

"I usually open," I answered immediately, not expecting the question.

"Great," answered Geoff, "since no one else is keen." I wondered what he meant and donned pads to accompany Geoff to the middle.

"You take the first ball as this lad is very quick," again made me think. At school, I had played for Ayr Cricket Club as an opener and faced some quick bowlers at age 17 with success and no fear of pace. That was on professionally prepared pitches, unlike the bumpy one I was standing on.

A tousle-haired youth charged in from a long run delivered a straight ball on a good length, and I confidently played forward with a straight bat. But, unfortunately, the ball landed on a bump at a fair pace and leapt in the air well above my bat, as I felt a crunch, and everything went black.

I seemed to see players at the end of a tunnel saying, "Give him room and air!" Strong arms got me back on my feet as I saw stars and choked on blood in my mouth.

Helped into the dressing room in a blood-stained shirt, I quickly came round and said I would resume my innings when I had cleaned up.

"You are not going anywhere except the hospital," said the camp doctor, holding up a small mirror from one of the wives' handbags. As I grinned back, I was astonished to see my front teeth clearly through a gap in my upper lip and a cut stretching up towards my nose.

37

The last time I was unconscious was playing school rugby, so my love of sport over the years cost me this incident, two broken fingers at cricket and a compound dislocated finger as a youngster.

My colleague, Jim, had already been taken to Truro for his tibial plate to be sorted, so I was taken by a car driven by one of the wives to Newquay. As I sat in my cricket gear in the waiting room at casualty, I was joined by a jockey from a local point to point, with a broken collar bone, again still wearing his riding colours, somewhat grass-stained in his fall.

After a short while, a heavily pregnant moaning young lady accompanied by her mother joined us. A nurse appeared, and we turned and pointed to the youngster.

"Not you again!" said the sister. "The doctor has told you twice today you are nowhere near started, so please go home and obey instructions!"

A local G.P. sutured my wound quickly and told me I had cracked teeth and should make a dental appointment. I told him a cricket ball which had hit the earth had caused my injury and enquired about antibiotics.

He answered he had cleaned the wound, and it would be fine. By now, I had a fair headache, and after my kind driver returned us to the cricket field, I thanked her. I could see that the demon bowler had almost finished off St. Columb, so I packed my kit and walked the short distance home slowly. Marie was surprised to see me back so early, and it was quite a few years till she relented about my cricket career.

Despite the doctor's confidence, the wound became infected and did not heal well, so I resorted to some doggy antibiotics, which did the trick but still left a scar and resulted in me growing a moustache to hide it.

Chapter Ten
Service Duty

No matter your occupation, the lowest in the pecking order usually gets the worst jobs to do. I found myself regularly given the monthly inspection of the guard dogs at the nearby R.A.F. airfield. Local rumour had it that nuclear weapons were stored underground there, and it was also a dispersal airfield for American bombers in case of war, hence the tight security.

On my first visit to the base, I was stopped at the main gate. Guards checked the car and made phone calls before I was searched, identified, and allowed to drive into the base.

The kennel block had an examination room built at one end, and I stood nervously awaiting beside a metal table. Finally, the handler appeared with the first German Shepherd, which crashed through the door dragging the handler at the end of a stout lead, and jumped up, placing large paws on the table. The dog panted furiously and eyed me suspiciously.

Sergeant Black stood efficiently to one side with pen and notebook introducing the patients. "This is Simba, sir! He has lumps on his arse, Sir!" he barked loudly and with military precision.

The handler did his best to help me lift Simba on the table, and I gingerly whipped a nearby muzzle off the wall and placed it over the danger end. I diagnosed a large anal gland abscess, and from my bag, retrieved a crescent-shaped scalpel blade designed for the procedure.

"Hold him tight," I instructed and pierced the lump. Pus shot satisfactorily over the table to the disgust of the Sergeant, whose uniform bore the brunt. All this was to the quiet amusement of the handler. This action, followed by an antibiotic injection, enabled me to predict a successful resolution of the problem.

"Take him out!" roared the Sergeant, quietly noting the wide grin of the handler as the dog dragged him from the room.

After a while, I had examined all the other dogs, which were fine, and although I was still intact, my nerves were in shreds.

"Only one left, Sir," said the sergeant, smiling broadly, which made the hairs on the back of my neck stand up, sensing danger. "Last is Satan, Sir - and be careful, Sir!"

This time a black long-haired German Shepherd dog crashed through the door with two handlers struggling alongside. "He has a swollen jaw and something wrong inside his mouth Sir," volunteered the handler in a shaky voice, which was the last thing I wanted to hear. Luckily the handler managed to get the muzzle on him, and I told the audience that it was a tooth abscess, and I would need to anaesthetise him, working on getting a sedative into the dog's back leg.

There was a small steriliser there, so I popped some instruments into it, including a small stainless-steel fret saw, which was with the dental tools I had brought with me just in case their use was needed.

Even with the sedative, it took three handlers to hold Satan as I administered Thiopentone into his radial vein, leaving the needle taped to his leg since I knew the anaesthetic might need to be topped up.

The upper carnassial tooth in the dog's upper jaw is enormous with three large roots, and with elevators, I loosened all three. Then I used the saw to cut down and separate the tooth in half, enabling me to extract it all.

Immediately pus poured out, and I turned my attention to the swelling in the side of his jaw, opening it with a scalpel then passing a probe through till I could see it emerge inside the mouth where the tooth had been. I gave antibiotics by injection and left tablets that were to be placed in Satan's food. I assured the horrified audience that, as far as I knew, no human teeth were similar.

Satan's handler grabbed my arm, saying, "Thank you, Sir! I love that dog, you know!" to the amazement of all present. After that, Satan was carried back by the two handlers, still unconscious, dreaming of eating vets alive!

Loosening my tie, I was glad of some fresh air outside. "Thank you, Sir! You did a brilliant job for a youngster. That Satan makes me sweat more than chef's curry!" said the Sergeant.

After I had packed up, he rang the gate, telling them what a great job I had done and that I was about to leave. This time I passed the gate without being stopped, and as all there saluted me, I felt a real sense of achievement.

A month later, there was a sad sequel when the Boss told me an urgent call from the Airfield on a Sunday afternoon.

I arrived to find a troubled Sergeant, who told me there had been intruders on the runway. One of the dogs had been sent out after them and had chased them to the wire. The interlopers had managed to climb out with great difficulty, with blankets over the barbed wire. The dog had stood there barking furiously and wagging his tail while the two intruders made off. The C.O. was furious and ordered the dog destroyed immediately.

When I enquired which dog was the culprit, the answer was Satan!

I arrived greeted by several handlers, who had already managed to get a muzzle on the condemned animal. As I approached holding the lethal injection, the brave handler insisted that he hold Satan, with all the present handlers visibly upset. This time Satan did not wake up.

Chapter Eleven
War Memories

Once a month, an elderly gentleman called Wing Commander Duggan would appear in the office as the Practice Accountant and try to make sense of the paperwork left by Boss Harvey.

One quiet afternoon I had to put some medicine inside the porch and wished to check on some details of a call I had done. So I went into the office that was filled with a pleasant aroma of St. Bruno tobacco. The elderly accountant sat there at work.

He smiled at me and said, "What a way to run a business!" pointing to an enormous beer pot that generally sat on the mantelpiece. "This is the petty cash!" he laughed as he counted coins and odd pound notes.

After stories from my grandfather and two great uncles who had served in the first world war, I had already started an interest in the subject and politely asked him where he had been stationed.

He was surprised at my interest and knowledge on the subject and spoke for half an hour about his experiences as a pilot in the Royal Flying Corps, which later became the R.A.F.

He seemed to enjoy my company, and from then on, I often made excuses to talk to him on Wednesday afternoons as he quietly spoke of flying over the trenches. He described awful dogfights and nights in the Squadron Mess, where riotous evenings were often spent, tinged by the fact that each day they all knew could prove to be their last.

It seemed incredible that this dear, kind old gentleman had killed several Germans in single combat and was upset to see their dying moments in burning planes plunging to the ground.

In 1918 he had hated orders to strafe trenches, realising the carnage he was causing, and still thought about what he had done decades later.

He enjoyed talking to someone who realised what he had been through and revealed he had told me more than anyone since, after the war, the subject was hidden in the minds of most survivors.

I was privileged to have known such an exciting and gentle friend.

Chapter Twelve
Four Brothers

One of the strangest places to call at was the farm of the Mitchell brothers, situated on the Newquay Road. I immediately knew I would be lucky to get away from the farm inside an hour as they were notorious for a good reason.

The four brothers were aged 60 to 80, usually comically dressed in tattered suits and gaiters. They ran the farm with no modern machinery and had draught horses instead of a tractor. The cows were hand milked, as they had no milking parlour, tractor or car, as none of the brothers had ever learned to drive.

They seemed to have a theory that if they asked for a call to one sick animal, they could ask for others to be looked at "While you be here!" So somehow, they thought that the bill would be less. This was, of course, not the case and only meant that more time than usual had to be allowed by Boss Harvey setting out a round of calls.

As I pulled into the farmyard, they all rushed towards me. The brothers had been all talking at once and constantly bickering with each other. The cow was treated the day before by Owen for milk fever and was again wobbly on her feet. Knowing that Owen would have advised taking as little milk as possible for a day or two, I asked if anyone had taken much milk from her.

"He did! I told 'im not to!"

"No, I didn't, Sir, 'ee did it!"

"You be a barefaced liar!"

Within seconds all four were involved in a heated argument, all shouting at each other. I ignored the chaos, went to the car, brought a further two bottles of calcium, and gave each something to do, which stopped the argument.

"In about 5 minutes, she should show some improvement after the intravenous bottle of calcium," I said, knowing what to expect.

"Well, Sir, while you be waiting, perhaps 'ee might 'ave a look at Tom as 'ee be a bit lame."

We all trooped to the stable where one of the Shires patiently waited, with a background argument, and several possible diagnoses were being bandied around. Then, finally, Tom allowed me to pick up his foot on the affected leg, and I immediately felt it warm and swollen.

I cleaned it up and pared a tender-looking area, and within seconds, black evil-smelling pus shot out from a hole revealed. I extracted a sharp piece of flint, gave a hefty dose of antibiotic and advised rest in a clean stable. "I knew it was that all the time!" started a new argument as most of them followed me to check the cow, who seemed to have made a significant improvement.

42

The fourth brother had now reappeared. He held a lamb in his arms, with a foreleg dangling, looking suspiciously like a fracture.

"When did this happen?" I enquired mischievously.

"Just this minute, Sir!"

"No! Twas yesterday!"

Ignoring them, I asked for a bowl of water and returned with a roll of plaster bandage. Then, with plenty of helpers to immobilise the leg, I carefully wrapped the Gypsoma around the limb and waited for it to dry, with my helpers holding the patient still.

"Pardon me, Sir, but 'ow is that bandage going to be strong enough to 'elp?" asked one, as the other three nodded their heads.

"In a few moments, it will be dry, and the chemical reaction will turn the bandage into a solid plaster cast," I told them all. "The broken bone will heal in three weeks."

My doubter had not finished yet. "What 'appens when we sell 'im, Mister?"

I told them I would return in three weeks to remove the cast, and they must check that the protruding foot did not swell up.

As I was washing my hands came, "While you be 'ere we 'ave a few calves need de- horning."

This time my patience had gone, and I told them to arrange it for three weeks **with** any other work needing doing, knowing very well that they would pay no attention to my request.

Rumour had it that one of the four did get married many years before, and on his honeymoon night, it was evident that his wife was already pregnant. So he dressed and shot out of the hotel, and his experience put the other three off going down the same road!

Chapter Thirteen
Holiday Accident

Every year as the holiday season neared, caravans appeared on the roads and traffic increased. Sometimes, it was so bad at the height of the holiday season that the police temporally closed Newquay, and on one occasion, on an emergency farm call, I was allowed through the queue with a police escort through the town.

This usually brought some mishaps to pets, and that side of work grew all summer. One early afternoon Owen and I were upstairs in the barn when we heard a loud shout for help down the stairs. We rushed down, and an estate car was parked below with the back open. A large black and white Border Collie was lying in the back of the vehicle. The tall young man was troubled and explained he had been walking along the cliff at Watergate Bay. The dog had followed another dog, lost his footing and had fallen over the cliff, a long way down, and could no longer stand.

We carried the collie into the consultation room, and I stared at the tall owner, just as he showed a flicker of recognition towards me. "Morton!?" I asked loudly, "It's me, Graham Watson from Ayr!"

"Graham! I'm sorry I didn't recognise you; it must be six years at least since I last saw you at Cambusdoon!"   We returned to concentrate on the beautiful huge collie in front of us.

I used a pair of artery forceps to press the dog's rear toenails with no response, and then needles pushed into his hip area and all around gave the same result. Owen also examined the dog, and while Morton was speaking quietly in his pet's ear, Owen turned to me and slowly shook his head.

"I am so sorry, Morton, but your dog's back is broken. He now has paraplegia and will never walk again."

I motioned to Owen, and we quietly left the little room as Morton sobbed inconsolably wrapped around his faithful collie's neck. In the barn, I explained to Owen that Morton had been a little older than me, but came from Ayr, went to Ayr Academy like me, and we played together at Cambusdoon, the home of Ayr Cricket Club, where he was a useful quick bowler who could also bat.

In those days gone by, I had memories of him walking around the ground with the handsome collie, perfectly trained, as his constant companion, and I knew the collie must now be elderly. I also knew that Morton was an officer in the Parachute Regiment and that the dog usually lived in Ayr with his parents.

After a few moments, we re-entered the room, and Morton had recovered his composure and gently asked if we would please put his pet to sleep. I asked Morton to hold him as Owen raised a vein, and I injected a hefty dose of Pento barbitone.

44

Leaving them together, we again left the room, Owen disappeared, and Morton finally came out.

I pointed and said, "All dead animals are buried in that field behind the house of my boss, by Leverton, our caretaker and gardener."

"I am so relieved," said Morton, "as I have a few more days here and could not possibly get him back to Ayr."

I made him a cup of coffee, and we had a chat about our good times at school and Ayr Cricket Club, and I established that his pet had had an incredible twelve years of life. He told me about his exciting life in the Paras, and we discussed the odds of the tragedy happening where it did, with the result that the vet present at the end had known them so well before.

"I am so grateful, Graham, and fate has meant he ended his life with two Ayr boys. I will never forget his wonderful life or your kind professionalism." He shook my hand and grabbed me as he shook with emotion and went slowly off on his sad way.

Throughout my whole career, I always found this the most challenging part of my occupation, and it never got any easier. The only compensation was to know that I was ending a bad or hopeless situation, a small crumb of comfort.

Chapter Fourteen
The Beginning

I arrived on the night of 27th February 1942, as brave British commandos spilt their blood, dismantling the new German Radar Station on the French coast at Bruneval. This other earth-shattering event took place at a Nursing Home in Ayr, Scotland, which has since been transformed, first into a garage and recently into a senior home, raising the possibility that I can terminate my life where it started! My dear mother Kit, all seven stone of her, took me back to my grandmother's cottage in Long Hill Avenue Alloway, a distance of 2 miles, passing the cottage birthplace of Robert Burns on the way, making me an official one-day-old "Honest Man."

My Grandmother, or "Gaggie," as I always called her, was tall, with a shock of pure white hair, which I later learned appeared in her thirties, a few days after the birth of a stillborn child. My grandfather had been a butcher in Ayr until he celebrated his success too much, and whisky brought about a premature demise, leaving my grandmother with six children. However, "Gaggie" was made of sterner stuff, and with the help of my mother (her eldest child), ran a guest house in Ayr for many years. Over the years, I have stayed several times on revisits to Ayr, an eerie experience.

My mother worked as a secretary in the nearby Ayr County Council building. She met my father, Jack, who worked in the Administration Department, and they had a courtship of seven years, saving up to get married when they could afford to buy a house. How times have changed!

This had now come to an end, and my father, Jack, had volunteered to join the Royal Artillery because of someone called Hitler, whose very name sent chills through my generation. With the start of WW 2, my mother decided that as my father was shortly off on active service, they should marry immediately after a seven-year engagement.

When I was a few months old, my father was posted to Scotland for mountain warfare training with his regiment. Father hired a cottage in Inverurie outside Aberdeen so my mother and I could be near him, and in December 1942, exercises took place hauling 25 pounder guns around the Scottish mountainside.

At Bridge of Brown, he led a convoy up a steep hill on a relatively narrow road. As acting Major, he was at the head of the convoy when a motorcyclist arrived at speed to tell him a Bren Gun Carrier had gone off the road near the end of the column. He jumped on the machine and headed back to find the carrier, partly off the road and on fire, raising the possibility of an explosion. Due to the situation of the vehicles, this raised the possibility of setting off a chain reaction up the closely packed guns, carriers and lorries loaded with live ammunition. No fire extinguishers were available, and he supervised a squad to heap earth on the carrier to limit the damage of an explosion. At the same time, the nearby vehicles were moved away with difficulty due to the steep hill and narrow road. Finally, he was satisfied and inspected the result, just as the carrier exploded, hurling debris and earth around.

My poor Dad was found in a field beside the road and carried into a nearby cottage while the convoy moved on until transport reached him. He remembers vaguely drifting in and out of consciousness in the place and besides a kitchen range. He almost fell off the stretcher as he was taken out of the cottage for treatment at the hospital.

In 1983 my wife Loraine and I found the cottage derelict but still there, and we stood in the kitchen, which still contained an old range.

Father was removed to Grantown-on-Spey cottage hospital where a young woman doctor rendered him first aid. He had multiple lacerations, burns, and fractures, an eye out on his cheek, and an almost severed right arm, so close to his shoulder that a tourniquet was impossible. As a last resort, she used a large needle to roughly sew through the muscle and skin as the only way to stop the bleeding.

The next day he was transferred to Raigmore Hospital Inverness, and their surgeons removed his right eye. His multiple lacerations and fractures were repaired, and the burns were treated. They tidied up the arm wound but were confident an amputation would be needed in a few days in the unlikely event that he survived the shock and blood loss.

Before the war, my father had been a civil servant and an excellent sportsman keeping goal at a high level in amateur soccer (in the running for an international cap), and at the young age of 26, captaining Ayr Cricket Club as a prolific all-rounder, in a team containing two Scottish internationals.

Due to his massive injuries, his life hung by a thread for several days until he miraculously started to improve. His subsequent recovery in the following weeks (including the arm) amazed the surgeons, who attributed it to his supreme fitness.

Eventually, my mother took me to see my father, encased in bandages resembling an Egyptian Mummy. He was agitated by this, even though I was too young to remember anything.

His extended stay in Raigmore Hospital, Inverness, took many long months and nineteen general anaesthetic procedures for his various injuries. At the same time, plastic surgery rebuilt his eye socket, and he was in a ward with several injured and badly burned R.A.F. aircrew.

His arm was attached to his abdomen. In time, the pedicle was attached to his head, till finally, the graft was left in place on his face.

Around this time, Noel Coward, the playwright and actor, made a morale-boosting visit to the hospital and played the saxophone perched on the end of my father's bed. But, unfortunately, due to the prevailing armed forces attitude to homosexuality at the time, his visit was greeted with stony silence and not a great success.

After many months my father returned home, but he was soon posted back to service. He joined an Anti-Aircraft Battery, Royal Artillery, in Kent for the remainder of the war.

His only thanks for saving the convoy from a fatal disaster was a regimental
enquiry into the loss of the Bren Gun Carrier. He was also sent a bill for losing his uniform, which was cut off in the hospital! If the incident had happened in Europe later in the war, he would probably have received a Military Cross.

His regiment was milked for 25 pounder crews for the desert war against Rommel. Then, after all the mountain training, they finally went into action at Walcheren in the battle of the Scheldt estuary in 1944, landing to fight ironically below sea level. Two Ayr Cricket Club teammates John Hunter and Gavin Girdwood, landed there as Artillery Officers in dad's regiment, and both were killed. They are buried in military cemeteries in Holland.

I was back with my mother at Alloway when my older cousins Ian and Allan came to stay, and my first memory of life is sitting on the back doorstep of the cottage. They were five and six at the time and had acquired a kitchen knife. They introduced me to the technique of digging up earthworms, cutting them into suitable pieces and eating them.
I recall enthusiastically joining in but not being too keen on the earthy flavour of the repast.
I was, of course, to spend my professional life dissecting creatures, but on future occasions, they hopefully felt less pain than the poor worms!

The next excitement in my life was our move to Belmont Place East in Ayr and the arrival of my sister Alison.

My father returned after the war with an artificial eye, which bothered me somewhat, especially when he took it out to clean it. However, he went back to work for Ayr County Council and tried to resume his sporting career. Goalkeeping was soon ruled out due to his restricted vision. At cricket, he found batting and fielding difficult but spent many hours in the nets perfecting a new technique as a spin bowler, and he was soon again playing regularly, and in future years, more than once took 100 wickets in a season.

Thus, my following memories are of the aroma of newly cut grass and crawling around beside the beautiful cricket field of Ayr C.C., called Cambusdoon, located in Alloway village. As soon as I could stand, I had a ball in my hand and played with the other small boys around the club.

One of them who lived beside the ground was Michael Denness, a good friend at cricket and Ayr Academy. On becoming a professional cricketer, he captained Kent and England for three years, including an Ashes series in Australia when England was terrorised by fast bowlers Lillee and Thompson.

If Michael had not become a professional cricketer, he was tipped to be a future fly half at rugby union for Scotland.

Chapter Fifteen
Ayr Academy

Fish came on Friday, as Ayr still had a fishing fleet, but the rationing of food was still present post-war, and very occasionally, we had a luxury day with a chicken which was a rare treat.

My mother made inventive cakes, and we didn't go hungry. The washed clothes hung on an apparatus hanging from the kitchen ceiling before going through the mangle, which was hard work for my mum, since she was so small, wearing children's shoes, as rarely could she get adult shoes small enough to fit her.

Growing up in the forties, Great Britain was in a poor state and had icy winters. As a small boy in town with my mother, I was fascinated by the war veterans. There were many limbless ex-soldiers with artificial legs that creaked as they walked, frightening me. Many were from the First World War and in their fifties and sixties, and some had dreadful facial scarring.

One that did upset me was a middle-aged man with a high double amputation of both legs. He propelled himself on a wooden board that had wheels, like a skateboard, using his hands.

In shops, he shouted his orders, and shop owners put them on his trolley and took his money.

Once a month, the coalman's lorry would arrive, with Alan Davidson painted on the front, and the coalman would unload, then sit on the back doorstep drinking tea and chatting to my mother, whom he called "Ma'am."

She always called him Davidson, and I told her I had been taught at school that the correct title was either Alan or Mr Davidson, and she was impolite. Mother said to me that he had been in the T.A. with my father. During the war, he was his batman. When he returned after hostilities to deliver the coal, she asked him to drop the formalities, and he refused, saying, "That won't do, as your 'usband will always be an officer in my mind, and will continue to be treated so!" Such was the social strata those days!

As my father was a keen cricketer, having recovered from his injuries, he still played cricket to a good standard for Ayr. I soon spent all summer weekends at Cambusdoon, a beautiful ground nearby Alloway just along Robert Burn's Cottage road. Occasional elegant houses surrounded it, and thick woods had Cambusdoon Private School on the other side, beside the imposing red-brick pavilion surrounded by white wood fences.

I would often spend days helping the West Indian professional Don Aitcheson, who doubled as a groundsman during the summer holidays. Every day in school holidays, he was supported by my fellow junior members, and our reward was some tuition in the nets.

50

He had a happy personality with a huge grin, and we worshipped him. I knew him better than most, as he lodged with my grandparents in Ayr. Then, having failed narrowly to reach the West Indian side, he decided to leave Jamaica and try his luck in Britain. My father met him in Glasgow as he alighted from the London train with several hundred passengers.

Seeing a solitary black person with a cricket bag, my father approached and said, "Mr Aitcheson?" The reply was, "How did you know me, man amongst all this crowd?"

During his five years at Ayr, Don loved telling this story against himself, always going into paroxysms of laughter about it!

When I was not at cricket in the summer, I would be on Ayr Beach, or the Low Green, a mile of flat grass behind the promenade where schoolboys endlessly played football, rugby and cricket all day, depending on the season.

Sometimes, it was off on our cycles to nearby villages and up Carrick Hill, five hundred feet high overlooking Ayr Beach, where we picnicked and played for hours.

I remember the horrible outbreak of myxomatosis in the wild rabbits, and we dispatched the worst poor blind miserable creatures with blows from sturdy sticks to prevent further suffering. I did not enjoy it or realise that it was my first effort in a long veterinary career.

Around the age of 10, I was fortunate to have a new class teacher, Leslie Hunter. He was younger than all my other teachers. Leslie had a very vibrant way of encouraging his pupils. As a result, the entire class was motivated like never before, resulting in thirteen graduates from a total of thirty pupils, a remarkable tribute to his abilities and something I have never forgotten. Leslie would eventually head a new College in Ayr, to the satisfaction of his former pupils who idolised him.

At the time, because of my artistic abilities, he encouraged me to consider a career as an architect. However, my thoughts already leaned in the direction of medicine, along with classmates Stewart and Isabelle. Later they both had distinguished careers in that field.

Eventually, I gained a place at Ayr Academy, and my education moved into a higher gear.

The school by the River Ayr was the oldest in Scotland and had an incredible staff who drove the pupils to achieve as much as possible. The mysteries of English Grammar, the terrors of mathematics, the fun of French taught by a dear old lady called Miss Bottomley, inevitably known to her pupils as "Wee Bummy!" The impossibility of Latin, led by another spinster very handy with the leather strap, was part of the day's routine.

The highlight of my days were sports periods, where we repaired to the gymnasium under the watchful eye of the school's sports master Captain T.B. Watson, held in admiration by those good at sport. However, he was significantly feared by those not of that inclination, whom he constantly pursued as "Malingerers."

Each day he would line up any claiming sickness to avoid physical education, and a typical parade would start like this:

"I have a cold, Sir."

"I've had a cold since the Somme! Get changed!"

"What's wrong with you, Sunnie?"

"I have a bad back, Sir."

A blow to the solar plexus would follow. "Now you have a bad front as well. Get changed!"

Noticing my surname one day, he asked if my father John had been a pupil, and when I confirmed this was the case, he informed me that if I were half as good a sportsman as my father, I would be fine - this gave me a great start, and my sports career at the school prospered.

Unlike today's situation, our school days were indeed happy. In the austerity of post-war Britain, we considered ourselves fortunate to attend such a fine establishment and were proud of the school, working as hard as possible and playing on the sports field as if we were fit to die for the cause!

Any pupil walking down the main street in Ayr, wearing a maroon Ayr Academy blazer, seemed to be regarded with admiration in those days. All the more so if you played sport in the school first team: you had a white edge added to the maroon colour. I was very proud to achieve this for cricket and rugby. I still have my blazer, and it still fits me!

Chapter Sixteen
Growing Up

Around the age of thirteen and during the summer holidays, John, Ian, Stewart and I cycled on a sunny day to Maybole, a nearby village with some steep hills in between. Ian volunteered to take our pooled pocket money into a nearby tobacconist shop, where he managed to purchase a packet of Wills cigars. We sat by the main road furiously puffing away and trying to look nonchalant and were disappointed at the only reaction being some giggles from a group of passing girls.

The way back in the summer heat made the hills seem twice as steep, and the result was all three of us enduring a spell of vomiting brought on by the cigars, a lesson I remembered for years to come and probably a fortunate one. The same friends accompanied me to Versailles's Ayrshire French Summer School via an appalling cross channel trip from Newhaven to Dieppe.

Halfway across, a gale, exceptional for the time of year, developed. The ferry was then forced to ride out the storm in mid-channel. Nearly everyone was seasick, though we somehow escaped the affliction. Amazingly we entered Dieppe the following day on a millpond sea. We entered the harbour with many poor souls prostrate on deck after their illness. I distinctly remember a very well-dressed French lady in an expensive fur coat rolling aimlessly on deck in her vomit, caring for nothing.

We stared at the scene of the disastrous wartime raid and proceeded to our rooms in a school dormitory near Paris. Trips to Paris and Versailles were impressive, but my main memories are twofold. First, a visit to a cafe in Versailles on some time out of reach of our teachers.

Ian was again the brave soul to order the bottles of white wine as Stewart and I sat outside the cafe basking in the sunshine. Many drinks later, we tottered back to sleep in the dormitory with about fifty beds. The following day I awoke with a very painful throbbing in my head and glued to the single sheet by a sticky offensive substance.

Horrified, I waited till everyone had gone to breakfast before skulking to the showers to sort out my predicament. Again, a lesson I remembered for years to come.

Another day we arrived in coaches in the middle of beautiful Fontainebleau Forest with a picnic. As we descended, a French girl who had been bugging me asked if I would like to go for a walk in "Zee" woods with her. I told her, "No fear," as I wanted to play football with my friends. In later years I was to wonder if I had made the correct decision.

Aged 15 years and still delivering papers, I was astonished to read one morning of a lad who played in my school rugby team. Since he lived on a farm, we rarely saw him, though he was in my year.

Living on the farm, he had driven a tractor for years. One day he took his father's Jaguar, and it was found the next day in a layby by the police. He had strangled his 15 years old girlfriend, then killed himself with his father's twelve-bore shotgun kept in the car's boot. We were astonished that he had a girlfriend, and there was no counselling at school in those days.

Chapter Seventeen
Hogmanay

I lived in a bungalow in a quiet but smart small street in Ayr, and my father was a senior local government officer with Ayr County Council. Our neighbours on each side of us were very reserved for three hundred and sixty-four days of the year, except Hogmanay or New Year's Eve.

We always held the party in our lounge. Many whiskies would be consumed, while our next-door neighbour always brought his father, who lived with the family. The elderly father was a retired shepherd. The father and son would choose every Hogmanay party to resolve differences of opinion that had been simmering for the past year.

When I was allowed to stay up in my later teenage years, I would often hear their voices grow louder and arguments start between them. One year the son pushed his father against my parent's glass cabinet, which was fortunately relatively empty for the only day in the year. The cabinet smashed open, and the elderly father responded by striking his son on the head with the fireside poker, amazingly with no serious result. My father calmed the situation, and the two spent the rest of the evening wrapped in each other's arms, consuming more whisky.

Every year at one a.m. there was a loud banging on the window, which heralded the entrance of Mr McConnell, usually clutching a flowerpot from the garden in one hand and a bottle of whisky in the other. He entertained us with dubious stories all night before staggering off home. Then, two days later, I would pass him in the street heading for the Glasgow train to his position as an accountant. He was dressed in an immaculate pin-striped suit, bowler-hatted, and with a copy of the Times under his arm. We would exchange a clipped "Good Morning" every time I saw him, which was the extent of our conversation until the next New Year performance!

Even in my younger years, we always had a family holiday, and in my early years, this was usually on a farm with gas-powered lighting. By now, I had a sister Alison, and the two of us would be out early collecting eggs in the hen house, and Alison's golden curly locks would be full of straw as we tumbled around in the hay lofts.

Helping to feed the animals was great fun, and the highlight of the day for me was a ride on the back of the tractor. In addition, I enjoyed farm life and was most interested in the animals, another possible early influence on my career.

My father's mother was English, and for many years, we travelled south to the family home in Godmanchester, a beautiful sleepy village near Huntington on the River Ouse. My great grandfather had been head gardener at a large riverside house in the lodge at the entrance drive, and his large family rented the house.   On his death, the sons and daughters finally owned it.

The house was constructed in the sixteenth century, with a garden stretching down to the River Ouse.   There was also a boathouse belonging to the large house. In the fifties, an attempt was made to build a bathroom with an indoor toilet on the side of the house. However, the wall was discovered to have been constructed with wattle and daub, resulting in the builders having to support the wall in a panic and building brick support.

My grandmother had five sisters and two brothers, and over the years, several combinations of them lived in this fantastic property. Unfortunately, only my Grandmother Winifred and her sister Constance married, and several sisters lost fiancées and boyfriends during the First World War.

My grandmother lived with my grandfather in Glasgow, where my father was born.   He had volunteered in 1914, followed by the two brothers.   She moved down with my father to Godmanchester for the duration of the war.

As a small child, my father attended a local primary school. It was a small building by the Chinese Bridge, a famous local footbridge over the gorgeous River Ouse (which still stands), and he well remembers his father and the brothers returning from time to time in uniform, sometimes wounded.

In nineteen seventeen, Connie married a Canadian soldier and left for a new life in Canada, never to return.

Four of the sisters lost boyfriends and fiancées in the war, and as a result, never married, but continued to live at the house with their two brothers Charlie and Tom. Charlie was shot in the arm at Monchy-le-Preux at the battle of Arras on Easter Sunday 1917, and I still have a letter he wrote describing his experiences at the casualty dressing station.

In 2011, I visited the area and stood in the field where the attack took place and where he was shot. The nearby cemetery is the resting place of many Bedfordshire Regiment men not so fortunate on that terrible day.

He recovered well enough to return to the Western Front only to be gassed in 1918.   On returning home, Charlie coughed so severely that till he died in 1945, he slept in a room made over the outhouse garden tool shed.   This was so that he would not keep the family awake at night with the noise of his coughing.

Tom served on the Somme, underage in the Bedfordshire Regiment, and survived a severe bullet wound in the thigh.   He did recover and worked after the war as a mechanic, eventually for Chivers in Huntingdon. A wild man, he never married, smoked, drank to excess, and terrorised the local women, and drove his sisters to distraction.

So badly did he treat them that Ethel drowned herself in the River Ouse at the end of the garden, and Rose gassed herself in the kitchen oven.

However, during my holiday visits as a young boy, he was my hero, and his extrovert character made him my favourite, making me laugh all day. One summer night, when I was around eight years old, he returned late evening from the pub. My sister and I were sleeping on blankets on the lounge floor. He woke me up, and the two of us set out to go fishing along the Ouse in the dark, in the rowing boat kept in the boathouse at the end of the garden.

As I put maggots on the hooks, he continued to drink the bottles of beer he had brought along. We fished until he fell asleep, and we drifted down the river in pitch darkness, and eventually, I decided that since I did not know where we were and could not swim, it was best to wait till dawn.

We awoke as the birds sang, and curious cows stared at us from the riverbank. Eventually, Tom revived, rowed us back, and we both crept back into bed, with my parents unaware of my adventure. Sadly, on his death, the house passed out of the family. However, I still love visiting sleepy Godmanchester and remembering my beautiful holidays as I walk past the causeway to the river.

As my years at Ayr Academy raced by, my parents kept up the pressure to study hard, though my father was still happy to see me do well at cricket and rugby.

By the age of fourteen, I was rising at six in the morning to do a paper round, which was a harrowing experience in freezing winter weather, and more than once, on windy wild days, I forlornly chased newspapers that had blown off my bike.

My original bicycle had belonged to a tall policeman and bought second hand, and my father made wooden blocks to fit over the pedals so my feet could reach them! So I slaved on my paper round and slowly saved enough to buy a second-hand Raleigh cycle with gears, which was my pride and joy.

I was starting to play rugby at school and had lost interest in soccer. Still, one summer evening, I was persuaded to join in a game at a nearby ground where the goals had nets, which was an irresistible draw.

I was appointed goalkeeper and enjoyed the game till a forward raced towards me on his own. Dutifully I rushed out to meet him, and he shot from close range as my hands went up in a reflex attempt at a close-range volley. Unfortunately, the ball struck my hand and hit the back of the net. I retrieved the ball and noticed that instead of my left index finger, I had a white bone pointing upwards, and my finger was bent back across my outer palm with a compound dislocation.

Having told my teammates that I could not continue, I went to the nearby main road into town and thumbed a lift to the Ayr Hospital casualty department. My finger was repaired under an anaesthetic nerve block and the tendons and skin sutured, which I watched with great interest.

This incident started an interest in the medical profession, which remained in the back of my mind for many years. Unfortunately, whilst this was happening, the game had finished, and my friends knocked on my front door to be confronted by my mother.

"Here are Graham's clothes, and we have put his bike in the garage as he is now in hospital," they announced, which shocked my mother rigid, and she was relieved to prise the detail that I had injured my hand.

On holiday in Cheddar in a caravan a week later, I was taken to Bristol Hospital by my father, and a doctor removed my sutures. He enquired how far I could now bend it, and painfully I moved it about half an inch. He then inquired, "Can't you do this?" and forcibly turned it right back to my palm, causing me to jump through the ceiling nearly. After that, I refused to go back to a doctor, and eventually, I had almost normal function restored, despite the efforts of Bristol.

No more than a year later, we had a great family holiday at the coastal resort of Charmouth, without me knowing that the area would figure in the rest of my adult life.

In 1940 as the German invasion was expected, my father, as a Captain in Royal Artillery, commanded a battery of 25 pounder guns on what is now the beach car park.

Every dawn, he patrolled the cliff on a motorbike watching for signs of parachutists or enemy ships. His fearsome armament was a revolver with no ammunition.

Hitler changed his mind about invading Lyme Regis Bay and had heard of my father's presence! (That was my father's story!).

On the way home from that holiday, we stopped in Manchester, and my father and I watched a Test Match where Ted Dexter played his first game for England.

Back at Ayr Academy, when I was about sixteen, I came round the corner of the dark corridor outside the art department and collided with another pupil, an incident that changed my life. The girl in question also took art and was in the year below me.

I stood for a second, staring into dark brown eyes almost hidden by almost black hair and a smile that made a great impression on me. During the subsequent few visits to the art department, I learned her name was Marie, pronounced "Maray", and I had met my first wife and mother of my children. Our school romance blossomed, though it proved somewhat fiery at times.

By now, I had become interested in a career in medicine and worked hard at my science subjects, including biology, soon a favourite subject. Morning assembly was a grand affair, with all pupils and staff present. The school orchestra played with my friend Stewart McCreath on lead violin

58

and the headmaster in gown and mortar board conducting assembly and morning prayers.

The upper school was on the balcony round the main hall, with junior years below, as a Prefect read a passage from the bible on the lectern beside the headmaster. I slowly lowered a dead frog from biology on a cotton thread onto the first-year girls' area below from the balcony above. A tremendous shriek split the air when it almost reached them, and the entire hall filled with laughter. The headmaster's face was scarlet with rage as he announced that all the pupils would remain standing all day if needed till the culprit walked down to his study door.

I duly did this while hundreds of pupils obediently stood in total silence as my footsteps echoed through the hall, and at the end of prayers, I was ushered into the great man's presence.

"Watson? I can't believe it is you! First XV rugby, captain of cricket, and senior Prefect!
What an appalling example to your fellow pupils." He then administered six blows on each hand with his leather strap, and I emerged in great pain, but with my reputation with my fellow pupils at an all-time high.

I had already experienced capital punishment throughout my whole secondary career, and it didn't ever bother me much. It was all part of life in those days and tended to produce discipline, though not always in my case.

I thoroughly enjoyed my life at Ayr Academy. The Scottish system at the time meant a substantial general education on every front possible. As well as our main subjects, information on mental arithmetic, ballroom dancing, table etiquette, everyday behaviour, respect for others, especially senior age groups, appreciation of the arts and music, and, of course, religion. It was a very different scene to the modern-day. I think it produced a balanced individual at the end, even though capital punishment was included and accepted as standard by the pupils.

I finally achieved Higher Certificate passes in eight subjects, a school record when three passes meant university entrance. The day before the last of my final school days was the annual prize giving, and I hatched a plot with my friends Ian, John and Stewart to leave a fire escape slightly open so that we could gain entry to the school after dark, before the prize-giving on the final morning.

Chapter Eighteen
Dodgy Behaviour

The headmistress was known as "Pussy" McWilliam, and her main task appeared to be keeping the opposite sexes as far apart as possible. Due to my romance with Marie, I was one of her prime targets. The plan was to erect a colossal notice we had painted in large letters on a sheet at the highest point in the main hall, where the annual prizegiving would occur. We had already found where the school ladders were kept, and at three a.m., we met in Ayr town centre, having climbed out of our bedroom windows.

We hid from the solitary policeman we encountered along the way and entered the planned fire door, which we had left slightly ajar. Armed with our little torches, we found the darkness inside the building quite overwhelming. The creaks of radiators made for a terrifying situation, not helped by occasionally bumping into each other with heart-stopping effect!

With some difficulty, we found the ladders. We climbed precariously to the highest wall on the second floor to place the sign as planned. We hid the school ladders in a different place, and we thankfully made our way back out and home by way of the windows to our respective bedrooms. I think if any of us had realised how frightening the escapade was going to be, none would have been so keen to volunteer. So, the break-in was achieved by a future headmaster, solicitor, orthopaedic surgeon and veterinary surgeon.

When we arrived together the following day for our final day at school, we were worried to see the caretaker at the school entrance and more alarmed when he gave the four of us a satisfied grin as we passed.

We saw that our sign, which was impossible to reach without tall ladders, had been removed from the hall. This event had occurred only minutes beforehand by the caretaker. He had scoured the town for a local builder to come at short notice with high ladders, the school ones still being hidden. Our disappointment was great since the sign read, "*PUSSY SAYS SEX IS GREAT!*"

During the summer holidays, I took various jobs to pass the time and earn some pocket money. My first job was helping at a local fruit farm. I arrived on the first day and was tasked with cutting lettuces with four other Ayr Academy pupils older than me. The foreman showed me how to cut a few, place them in a barrow, then move on a few feet. As soon as he was gone, my companions pointed to a second barrow concealed nearby and told me to put every sixth lettuce there.

The field was full of pupils of all ages working away, and when the rogue wheelbarrow was packed, a pupil two years older than me collected it and took it to a hole in the hedge at the corner of the field. Then, once a day, a mysterious van appeared, and the pile of vegetables disappeared.

No one had difficulty arranging my silence since the pupil organising this was my hero, being a top rugby and cricket star at school and singing in the choir at my church.

His name was Ian Ure, and he went on to play soccer for Dundee, Manchester United, and captain Scotland in a team with Jim Baxter, Dennis Law, and David Gibson (who would play golf with me in my retiral). In the same year was Mike Denness, who captained England at cricket. In my year and Academy first XV was Ian McLauchlan, who captained Scotland at rugby, and was a British Lion and President of the Scottish Rugby union for many years.

My next two years saw me land a fantastic summer job as a greenkeeper at the Ayr Belleisle Golf course. I started cleaning toilets and cutting greens with a hand mower, backbreaking work, especially after rain.

However, by my second year, I had graduated to easy jobs like raking bunkers and driving the pre-war Massey Ferguson tractor towing the gang mowers on the fairways.

Apart from the stench of paraffin, the danger of being hit by golf balls (no safety guards those days), the front offside wheel would come off at some stage every day, and I would be propelled onto the grass.

The head greenkeeper was summoned, and he lifted the axle while I repositioned the wheel and screwed the bolts back on. Of course, being over six feet tall and massively built, the ex-Desert Rat Sergeant Major found this no problem, and I didn't dare complain that the event was inevitable the following day.

A consolation was the occasional game of golf with my friends with borrowed, shared clubs, and no tickets, on the number two course at Seafield. One of the group would keep an eye open for the approach of the ticket collector, and we would then run off faster than he could! Fifty years later, I played on the same course, and when I told the ticket officer that it was the first time I had paid for a ticket, he stared at me in disbelief.

Chapter Nineteen
Cornwall Continued

John had always wanted to be a farmer.   His father had been a farm labourer, and John had studied at Agricultural College, working hard for his qualification.   Tall and handsome with a shock of black hair, he had worked on dairy farms for several years, and his parents had died, leaving their house to their only son. The capital allowed John to go to the bank for help to buy local Barton Farm, which had been on the market for some time.

I met him coming out of the bank, dressed smartly in a suit, with his pretty wife dangling on his arm, and they could hardly wait to tell me that they had got Barton and would start a new dairy herd very soon. I liked John and was so pleased for them both, wishing them well.

Over the next year, the run-down farm was entirely transformed by their hard work, and a dairy parlour and all new equipment were installed. In addition, there was a steady increase in the number of cows each year. I enjoyed my occasional visits to John and May, with a Border Collie wagging its tail beside them.   John knew what he was doing, worked so hard, and the future looked promising.

One June day, I drove down his track, past a newly painted sign announcing Barton Friesians with his name below and found he had done it himself with an excellent likeness of a Friesian cow.

As usual, his barking collie pursued me, nipping at my tyres into the yard, and on my arrival greeted me by jumping all over me in delight. John had trouble with a calving heifer and led me into a new loose box he had built himself. The tail of almost certainly a dead calf was evident, and John told me he could not bring the legs up to the birth canal.

May stood ready with warm water, soap and a crisp, clean towel which would have looked good in the best hotel in Newquay. Stripping to my waist, I lathered up and confirmed the situation and prepared an epidural anaesthetic.

"This will cause a nerve block to stop the contractions," John announced to May, whose eyes were like saucers.   I clipped the hair and cleaned an area at the end of the patients back before inserting the needle into the spinal canal. May handed me the syringe of local anaesthetic, which I gave, making the heifer's tail go floppy.

The patient chewed some hay and lost interest as I located the legs, and we pulled out a dead calf that did not smell too nice.

It was hard to watch their disappointment, and I took the offer of a coffee after I had cleaned up. "That is the third heifer this year to have a dead calf, all by Parkin's young bull," said John. "Perhaps he's no use?"

"Have you had any heifers losing calves early?" I quietly asked.

May replied that they had two heifers, "slip calves after a thunderstorm," which sent alarm bells ringing in my brain.

"John, if you get the two heifers in next week, I will come up and give them a blood test, just to make sure they are o.k.," I said, trying to sound quite casual.

John seemed happy with that and told me how despite this minor setback, he was hoping soon to expand the herd and take on a cowman to assist him, preferably a youngster who had also been to college.

"Nothing against the older generation, but farming is changing fast, and you have to plan for the future." As I drove back, I wished more of my farm clients had the same attitude instead of being suspicious of all new treatments.

I took some blood from the heifers a few days later, with John as cheerful as ever. Then, a week later, I returned from my round, and as I walked into the office, Boss Harvey handed me a letter saying, "You had better take a look at this!"

My horrified gaze read Barton Farm, two heifers positive for Brucella Abortis.

"Oh no!" was all I could gasp, knowing that Brucellosis was an increasing problem in Cornwall. It was a contagious bacterial infection causing abortions and dead calves and could even transmit to humans.

After finishing my round that afternoon, I headed straight for Barton Farm. As we met in the yard, John recognised my expression and asked, "Brucellosis?"

"I'm afraid it is," I replied as we walked in silence to the house.

We spent the next hour discussing a damage limitation strategy while a silent May sat at the table, head in her hands with tears streaming down her cheeks. Over the next few months, my unofficial visits became more frequent, and John's depression grew more profound. Several more calves had been born dead, and things looked grim. John's cheerful manner had gone, and he looked pale and drawn.

My next visit found an empty yard, and as the back door was open, I entered the kitchen calling out their names. May appeared from upstairs, saying that John was not well, and the doctor had just left after diagnosing flu, saying John must stay in bed and that she was struggling to milk the cows on her own.

I climbed the stairs to find a poorly John sweating in bed in a pair of striped, blue pyjamas.

"I wish you had some medicine for me," he tried to joke, explaining how it was challenging to milk the cows with a splitting headache. I tried to console John and left. On my way home, I stopped at Bramble Cottage, more a house than a cottage with lovely gardens, and the home of Dr Holt.

Since it was now 7.30 p.m., I found him tending his roses and puffing his pipe in the garden. "Hello, Mr Vet," he joked, and I replied, "Hello, Mr Doctor!" in our usual greeting, which we preferred in the Red Lion.

"Martin, I know you visited John at Barton Farm today."

"Yes! Unusual to see such bad influenza in a strapping lad like him."

"Did he mention that his heifers are infected with Brucella Abortis?" I asked. After a silence, Martin replied that John had not mentioned that.

"Please don't think I'm questioning your diagnosis, but my textbooks mention the possibility of recurring flu-like symptoms occurring in humans caused by Brucella."

"Sorry Graham, I had not heard of that. I will get some blood from him tomorrow and send it to Truro Hospital. Anyway, come indoors and have a beer." I followed him into the lovely old house, and we spent a pleasant half-hour together. I told him I felt awkward as a junior assistant having to question a senior doctor's diagnosis.

In Martin's usual friendly way, he reassured me, telling me he was grateful to me for bringing it to his attention and advised me never to refuse help and always to keep an open mind over every case.

"How serious could this be?" he asked.

"Very much so, I'm afraid. The herd milk yield is down, and with so many heifers having lost their calves, there will be few replacements for older cows next year. I happen to know John has a sizeable bank loan and is not able to stand significant losses. I am, of course, telling you this in confidence so that you are aware of his situation."

"Thanks, Graham, all logged-in old boy!" said Martin as we stood up. He shook my hand as I walked to the door. As the months went on, dead calves continued, and the milk yield stayed low.

Martin had rung me to say John had been diagnosed with Brucellosis, which could cause recurring bouts over the years, similar to Malaria.

My unofficial visits continued, and each day I was greeted by Meg jumping on me and licking my hand furiously. Then, one day I heard banging noises in the barn and found John trying to repair his tractor, with a pale face and sweat dripping on his forehead.

"Got to try to fix it myself," he chirped, "as I can't pay a mechanic anymore, and the bank is hounding me!"

Over time things did not improve, and I marvelled at John's strength of character and constant cheerfulness as his troubles mounted, and I grew to dread calls to Barton Farm since I felt powerless to help.

Having kept Mr Harvey informed, I felt pretty emotional one day when he quietly told me that he had not been charging for my unofficial visits.

"You are a kind, thoughtful soul," I blurted out, leaving the room in a hurry. Later that year, when all was lost, John committed suicide in the barn.

Chapter Twenty
Happier Days

My friendship with Owen and his wife Charlotte was exceptional, and one Saturday that we were both off duty, they asked Marie and me for Supper. Charlotte was a lovely, intensely shy person in those days, though she was very bright and similarly qualified to Owen and me as a dentist. She worked hard for her first-ever dinner party, and Marie and I joined them in the lounge, all of us in smart clothes.

We had a pleasant few drinks beforehand, with Charlotte popping off occasionally to the kitchen, and nearby dining room, separated from us by folding doors. Eventually, she announced that the first course was ready, and Owen parted the doors to reveal the lovely room with candles burning romantically near the table.

The first course was pate, and in the dimly lit room, frozen motionless on the table, stood their mischievous Irish Setter, having just finished off the last off the pate. He seemed to have the idea that if he stood still in the dim lighting, he would be invisible!

Three people were in hysterics of laughter, while Charlotte appeared close to a nervous breakdown. Finally, Owen and I did the sensible thing and retreated to the lounge for another drink. At the same time, Marie helped Charlotte clear the table before we continued to the main course, and even Charlotte finally enjoyed the evening. The poor soul would never be allowed to forget the occasion!

I would hate to think how many times in my career my social life has been invaded while on weekend duty.

Now John was old enough to have a babysitter, and we were fortunate in having a kind lady nearby who enjoyed looking after him. A Saturday evening saw us just leaving for a barbecue when the phone rang. "My dog's been sick all day, and now I think he be dying!" exclaimed Mr Balfour, a client in the village whom I seldom saw.

I replied that I would meet him if he came straight to the practice premises. So Marie and I went straight there and opened the premises, which was hot in the early evening sunshine. I passed the time rummaging in the sizeable old file box of small animal records, finally locating the form which showed the bitch had an emergency hysterectomy a year before (also on the weekend!) After waiting for half an hour, I paced around outside, with my demeanour rapidly worsening.

Marie appeared to join me and revealed she had just rung Mr Balfour and learned that his dog seemed better, and he was not bothering to come after all. "**What!** I don't believe it", I shrieked, racing in towards the telephone, which rang as I approached it. Expecting Mr Balfour, I was just about to tell him what I thought of him when I found another emergency call was on the way.

I rushed out to find Mrs West with an aged collie in her arms, accompanied by a hysterical teenage daughter. Grasping the comatose dog called Meg, I carried her into the consulting room.

They had just found her unable to stand, and her head was to one side with staring eyes flicking from side to side. Establishing that Meg was now 15 years old, I told them that she had suffered a severe vestibular problem and was unlikely to recover, particularly with her respiratory distress.

"No! No!" screamed the daughter, draping herself around the poor patient. Mrs West immediately agreed to euthanasia and tried to calm the daughter. As I prepared the lethal injection and Marie held up the radial vein, I turned to the daughter, asking if she would help me by talking gently in Meg's ear. Having something to do calmed her down, and the poor dog went peacefully off to sleep.

I found a blanket, wrapped Meg in it, and placed her gently back in the car since Mrs West wanted to bury her in their garden.

As they prepared to leave, the car window wound down, and the daughter leaned out in my direction. Shaking with red-eyed emotion, she blurted out, "Thank you, thank you. You are a wonderfully kind man." She grabbed my hand and kissed it.

As they drove off, Marie turned to me, saying, "Come on, Superman, let's get to the party!" The idiotic Mr Balfour was now long forgotten.

On one farm visit to see a cow, the farmer Mr Tremaine asked me into the house to look at a duck they had. It had become so tame that it frequently came into their kitchen in inclement weather and was like a pet.

However, Marmaduke suddenly could not walk on one leg. I checked him and, finding a clean fracture, managed to put a small plaster cast on the leg. In the day book, I wrote the farmers name saying "Duck when passing."

As we assembled the following day in the office, Boss Harvey started the proceedings by asking, "Has someone had a problem at the Tremaine farm?" At first, everyone, including me, was baffled till he read out my note in the book. Then, I think he assumed someone had made a costly error, and the farmer was watching out at the farm entrance with his twelve bore shotgun!

Working in my region of Cornwall was a magical experience, with the winding lanes, small farms all very different, and the nearby holiday beaches, with the Padstow harbour particularly beautiful and unspoiled in those days.

Around this time, Maria and I looked at a cottage in the Padstow area priced at £900. In those days, owners could park outside. We decided it was too early to attempt a mortgage, and I sometimes wonder what it is worth today?

We had, on the bank managers advice, to look at life insurance for me now that I had a wife and son. So an appointment was made for a representative to call regarding this.

However, that day I had an emergency call and left Marie to deal with the visit of the insurance agent. First, he sat beside her on the sofa and explained all about the policy. Then, sitting close to her and explaining the details, he suddenly put his arm around her.

Before she could react, the ordinarily placid Tim flew across the room and inflicted a nasty bite on his arm, causing him to vacate the premises quickly. We used another firm for the policy.

Chapter Twenty-One
Changing Times

Over the next two years, another assistant, Peter Hill, joined the practice. Peter and his wife Kate were very friendly, with Peter having a quiet nature and Kate more outgoing.

As usual, he was paired at first with Mr Harvey for evening duties. Unlike Boss Harvey, an amiable gentleman, Mrs Harvey considered herself of a particular station. She did have a cook who also did all the cleaning in the large Penmellyn house. Amazingly, everyone, including her husband, called her by her nickname "Froggy."

She called everyone, including the veterinary assistants by their surnames, and she finally met her match in Kate, during an incident a few weeks after Peter started work.

Peter was on a call with Boss Harvey, who had gone out late at night to a wealthy equine client, and he had unusually undertaken a night call.

A calving call came in at 2 a.m. The call was taken by Mrs Harvey, who immediately called Peter, who was sleeping soundly.

Kate answered the call, and Mrs Harvey boomed out, "I want to speak to Hill!"

Kate answered, "I beg your pardon Mrs Harvey, whom did you say you wish to speak with?"

"Hill, Hill, I need him *now*!"

"Well, Mrs Harvey," replied Kate, "You may speak to Mr Hill or Peter, whichever you wish to ask for."

A stunned silence followed, so Kate repeated her statement, and after a long period of quietness, Mrs Harvey reluctantly asked to speak to Peter.

The story was a sensation among us the following day, and we were astonished when Mrs Harvey started calling each of us by our Christian names. We wondered if she noticed the more helpful and friendly way we responded to her in future and always wondered if Boss knew what had happened?

Within a year, Peter and Kate left the practice to take up a Commonwealth post with the Ministry of Agriculture in the then British Honduras, a British colony in Central America, now Belize. Peter had a fantastic collection of butterflies and was hugely interested in wildlife conservation, in an age when little was known about it, and this had influenced his decision.

We were sorry to see them go, and when they arrived by ship, Peter saw a gentleman on the harbour wall who was holding a sign saying "Peter Hill".

He approached him and politely asked to be taken to the Chief Veterinary Officer. "You are the Chief Veterinary Officer!" was the reply, which shocked him, and their adventures in the next two years would fill several books, I am sure.

Peter was replaced by Angela, a bright and very clever single vet, who quickly slotted in well, though she did have a hard time convincing farm clients of her abilities!

Boss Harvey bought a house for her in St. Merryn, halfway to Padstow, and a little small animal consulting room was started there.

As I ended my second year, I began to think about what would happen in the practice when Mr Harvey retired.

I was aware that Dixon and Owen were ahead of me in the pecking order. In addition, one of Mr Harvey's sons was halfway through his course at London University studying to become a vet, making a further complication.

Realising I had little chance of becoming a partner, and I was not too keen on Boss Harvey's son, who came with us on farm rounds during the summer holidays, made me think hard about the future.

The first time I took the student son out with me, I examined a cow and told the farmer what we must do. I then invited young Harvey to check the cow himself. He disagreed with my diagnosis! The farmer accepted mine, and as I was cleaning up afterwards, I heard young Harvey lecturing the farmer on feeding the cow incorrectly. As I left, the farmer winked at me, and we went in silence. Then, a little way down the farm track, I stopped the car.

Turning to my companion, I said, "Let us get one thing straight. I am the vet, and you are a student!" So we continued the round in silence, and he did not come out with me again for some reason.

I decided that my prospects of ever becoming a partner in the practice were very remote. So I searched the Veterinary Record for fresh posts, having interviews in Rotherham, Coventry and Nuneaton. But, unfortunately, none of the posts appealed to me, especially after the beautiful Cornish countryside and my home town of Ayr.

Posts in Scotland were very few, and I continued my search in England, finally going for an interview at Stourport on Severn.

I was particularly interested since Roger Vale, and the senior partner, was a kind, gentle character who explained that he had started the practice in a large house on the outskirts of Stourport, mainly doing large animal work. He had now moved house himself, and Eric Smith, one of his partners, had moved into his large house. There was a vast garden, and they had sold the land for a new housing development on the edge of town. With the proceeds, the three partners had built new surgery premises with a good car park. They hoped to encourage the development of small animal work, hoping that if I could build up this part of the business, I could soon become a partner since none of them was very interested in treating small animals.

With my Brucellosis problem (In Cornwall, I had been diagnosed with Brucellosis causing a persistent skin infection on my arms. Calving cows

69

did not help this with no protective gloves in these days), and I would do less and less farm work, this seemed an ideal opportunity since Stourport was near Bewdley on the River Severn and was surrounded by pleasant Worcestershire countryside.

One of the new houses in the development next to the premises would be for me, so the set-up seemed ideal, and Marie was also happy to go there to a brand-new house. It was a sad day when I told Boss Harvey I intended to leave, and he seemed genuinely upset.

Just as I was leaving, he had taken Dixon as a junior partner at St. Columb, and it still left Owen as an assistant with Angela. Then, incredibly within a year, a dreadful incident occurred.

Angela was at the St Merryn house and branch surgery talking to Owen. Seeing their cars, Boss Harvey stopped on passing and walked into the lounge, where they were enjoying a quick coffee. To their astonishment, he sat down on the floor, leaned against the wall, smiled at them and died!

They tried to revive him, and a doctor appeared very quickly, but a massive heart attack had been the end of our much-respected Boss.

The upshot was that while making Dixon a junior partner, a clause had been inserted saying that if either partner died, the other had the opportunity to acquire the rest of the practice.

I understood that Dixon spoke to Owen and Angela, who went to the bank and raised the capital to buy into the partnership with Dixon. If I had stayed another year, it would probably have included me.

Mr Harvey's son was therefore never offered a chance to join his father's practice.

In my time in Cornwall, I had a fantastic, exciting start to my career. This followed my first impressions while seeing veterinary work in Ayr, then my five years of intense education at Glasgow University.

Inevitably my career saw massive changes in the profession over my forty-one years in different kinds of practice.

My schoolboy introduction was in practice geared almost entirely in farm and equine practice. Though household pets were seen and operated on, the young assistants invariably did the work, as the partners seemed to consider treating small animals as an increasing nuisance!

At that time, I was still delivering newspapers from a shop on Ayr beach seafront, and every early morning I would see an elderly gentleman ride a large grey mare along the two-mile beach. Three border terriers always ran alongside, and it fascinated me when the little dogs ran underneath the mare on wet days, somehow avoiding being trodden on but keeping dry. One day I was told this was Mr MacGregor, the retired former head of the vet practice I would soon attend as a schoolboy.

When I started in Cornwall, the farms were primarily small mixed farms, often with a few cows, sheep, pigs, and the farmers rarely attempted any treatment themselves. Sick animals meant an immediate call for the vet to help. The advent of antibiotics and steroids alone had an enormous impact on the armoury of the vet, and farmers were often amazed at cures, impossible not too many years ago.

Much of the farm work was carried out as it had been for centuries! As a young vet, I castrated young calves and piglets surgically with no anaesthetic. I remember spending a morning burning tails off lambs with a red-hot iron, kept hot in a brazier beside me, with no pain killer at all, which I did not enjoy.

Horses were castrated by casting them with side-line ropes, then using a mask with Chloroform! Amazingly the results were good.

At the time, cats brought in for castration were given Thiopentone by i/v injection. However, frequently while doing farm calls in Cornwall, a tom cat would be caught, stuffed head downwards into a wellington boot, and with the farmer holding its back legs, I would castrate him in a few seconds, before he was released, and shot across the farm yard to hide!

Although Brucellosis was a problem, the vets calved cows stripped to the waist, and no protective gloves were used then.

Continuous Thiopentone intravenously was the only small animal anaesthetic used in the practice and a mask with ether for occasional rabbits. We had no x-ray facilities, and blood tests were few, mostly on cattle for infectious diseases like Brucellosis. No calving traction machines were available, and if normal calving with ropes was impossible, the only resort was a caesarean.

Veterinary practice during my forty-one years gradually changed from mostly farm and equine work, or large animal practice as it was called, through to mixed practice. Large and small animal work was shared here equally, such as Stourport, to small animal practice entirely. Throughout my career, I had moved through all of these combinations, which was unique.

In 2020, practices of various kinds still existed. Still, the vast majority treat domestic pets only, and nowadays, many more exotic species are included, which was not the case in my years.

Another change in more recent years is the development of vets who specialise in different aspects of one species. So, for example, there now are many Equine specialists, and so on for all species and specialists in various aspects for one species.

You can now refer a dog to an ophthalmic specialist or refer a herd of cattle to a vet specialising in infertility problems. But, of course, such a scenario would have been unbelievable to Mr Harvey, my much-admired first boss.

The veterinary profession has significantly benefited from advances in the medical field, following into the veterinary field. In the same way, it is now possible for qualified veterinary nurses to specialise in, say, orthopaedic work. In addition, all vets have to undergo a specified number of days learning about new developments to update their knowledge constantly.   All of these developments would have been unheard of in my early days in practice.

Chapter Twenty-Two
Glasgow University

At Ayr Academy, I was interested in medicine after reading books about Sir Bernard Spilsbury, the father of modern forensic medicine. I felt that was a career in which I was interested. However, on reflection, I worried about how I would cope with being a consultant of any kind. As a medical G.P. did not appeal to me, I started to look at alternatives, especially veterinary medicine, where an exciting career looked possible with more variety than a G.P. doctor.

In my final school year, I approached the local veterinary practice and was accepted to watch the work taking place during my school holidays. This allowed me around the premises to observe and be taken out in the countryside to see farm animals and horses treated. To receive this privilege, I washed endless cars and cleaned and polished continuously, being terrified of the tempers of the senior partners.

I managed to stay upright on my first day whilst watching a major operation on a cow and started to dream of a future as a vet. Gradually I began to make sure I went out with the younger vets. Ian Drummond and Jim Begg showed me kindness and encouraged me to apply for Glasgow University Veterinary School entrance.

One day Jim Begg and I went out to de-horn an adult Ayrshire bull, which involved injecting a local anaesthetic into the side of the head before sawing off the horns with a butcher's saw. We expected the bull to be tied up in a stall in the long indoor building where we were both directed, where the cows spent the winter months.

To our astonishment, the doors opened at the other end, and the bull appeared. It was being prodded into the building with pitchforks by the farmer and helpers.

As we stood in the gangway surrounded by equipment, Jim whispered calmly to me, "If I were you, I would plan your escape route now."

Within seconds we were both hanging from the wooden rafters above us. The bull passed underneath at full speed, trashing our instruments, and crashed straight through the shut doors at the other end of the byre into the field beyond. We abandoned the attempt, and I made sure I did not attend the repeat visit.

Nevertheless, I spent many weeks there and managed to stay on my feet when I watched my first farm operation.

In those days, hay bales, now tied up by string or baler twine as it is called, were held together by wire. Occasionally, a piece of wire left in a bale would be swallowed by a cow and pierce the bowel, causing peritonitis. Many of these, though, would stay in the bottom of the cow's largest stomach, the rumen, without causing harm, till the cow died.

Later in my student career, I had seen many cow's rumens opened at abattoirs, and items of metal of all kinds, even tin cans, were often present.

Sometimes, however, the wire pierced the wall of the rumen, leading to infection and pain, the danger of severe illness, and inevitable death. This was usually quickly diagnosed by pressing the middle of the cow's back, which caused extreme pain, and the cow would emit a hefty grunt. The practice did have a wartime mine detector which was also used, but a ping without pain meant nothing for the reason I have given and could even give a false positive if a spade or metal object was nearby at the time.

An epidural and local anaesthetic would be given, and as a worried spectator, I watched skin, muscle layers, and finally, the peritoneum opened. The rumen occupied all of the exposed space, making an incision into it easy. A terrible odour surfaced, caused as the fermentation process to digest grass fibres took place (something humans cannot do!) The odour was appalling and much worse than the surgery.

The vet reached the bottom of the rumen till he felt the sharp piece of wire and pulled it out. It then only remained to close the wound and give an antibiotic injection to prevent any peritonitis.

Apart from the terrible odour, I had enjoyed watching it. Moreover, since Ian, the other young assistant, did the surgery, he allowed me to give the antibiotic injection, which was a big thrill and made me more determined to become a vet.

Eventually, after being interviewed among hundreds of prospective students for a place in the annual intake of forty at the Glasgow Veterinary School, I was amazed to be accepted but nervous about leaving home comforts for the perils of city life.

I arrived for my first morning at Glasgow University terrified. After a short welcoming talk from a lecturer, forty-four of us were left drinking coffee and introducing ourselves. Less than half were Scottish, and I began talking to them before noticing a group of English boys in a corner, laughing loudly, surrounding another English lad who seemed to be speaking a lot! After a while, I went over to the instigator of the hilarity and discovered his name was Dai Davies. Immediately I had become acquainted with the individual who was to become my partner in crime and a lifelong good friend.

Some of our first lectures were shared by medical students in the old Victorian lecture theatres in the main University buildings, where around 200 students in raised seating to the roof awaited the unfortunate lecturer. First, he was greeted by a deluge of two hundred paper darts. This was followed by glass marbles coming noisily down the steps.

Occasionally, Stewart McCreath (ex Ayr Academy), a medical student, played his violin whilst lying on his back in the tallest row of seats.

Despite this mayhem, the Botany lecturer carried droning on without moving a muscle and calmly left after an hour of being ignored. So we suffered this subject, to get used to learning boring facts, to help us later to study anatomy.

It wasn't long before we moved to the old vet college in Buccleuch Street, a decrepit building once a large stable for Glasgow Police horses. We started anatomy on the lower floor, which facilitated the entry of animal carcases stored in formalin in large vats, like pickled onions!

Each morning we began the task of operating chains to remove them for dissection, wearing white coats which became more soiled as the day went on. Inevitably the four girls out of the forty-four students in my year, at some stage every day, would attempt to find a handkerchief in their pocket and instead find a suitable piece of an animal reproductive organ.

Talking of anatomy, I had to find the address of a future Saturday party from the Stewart as mentioned above one day. Therefore, I crept through the door of the human anatomy building into a hall with two hundred students dissecting numerous dead bodies that were all of black origin.

Stewart explained that, at that time, all the bodies available mainly were foreigners who had been executed. He introduced his unfortunate cadaver as George and produced a biro from George's nostril to write down the address of the Saturday party!

As students for five years in a small class of forty-four, we all became close friends. Soon I was with four classmates, including Dai, Alasdair, Peter and Hugh, in a tenement flat at Gibson Street close to the University Union building, where we took turns cleaning and cooking with no great success.

By this time, my sister Alison had become a student nurse at the nearby Western Infirmary. Every other Saturday morning, she and some friends arrived. They insisted we leave the premises and attempted to make the flat more sanitary. We were happy with this arrangement which allowed my fellow students to ogle the nurses, and no doubt some of them were able to contemplate the idea of landing a vet for a husband. The downside was attempting to get into our bed that Saturday evening, which was almost impossible. The girls had made up the beds in sixties hospital-style. Sometimes this did not help the aspirations of my flatmates with a female friend brought back from the Student Union dance!

We had to work very hard. The winters were freezing, but we had a wonderful and hilarious five years, playing sport and dealing with permanent insolvency. This was caused mainly by spending too much money on excessive quantities of beer in the Union beer bar each weekend. Friday night saw the vet college dance each week, and Dai and I soon had some responsibility for running it.

We inherited a decrepit trio playing ballroom music, and attendances were poor. However, we were interested in the pop music explosion and soon hired a sixties-style band playing Rock and Roll. They were called "The Thunderbirds." There now had an unforeseen consequence of leading to a music revolution on the Glasgow student scene. As a result, attendances became significantly oversubscribed, causing problems on the door. Non-vet students were charged, while vet students were not. Vet students were also allowed in when we were officially full.

This had near-tragic consequences one evening when trouble erupted following some non-students being turned away. At the end of the dance, I left with Dai and others in the dark outside, and a mob attacked us.

Also present was a student in the year below us, Jim Wight, who received a blow to his jaw. He was the son of Alf Wight, later to become famous as the author of the James Herriot books, which resulted in a renowned T.V. series All Creatures Great and Small.

The troublemakers did not realise that one of my classmates, Clem, a superb rugby player and renowned man of the world, was also with us. In seconds he had landed blows on them, causing their immediate withdrawal from the scene.

We all piled into Dai's old Zephyr to drive to a party, as in those days, there was no breathalyser to cause us to worry. Unfortunately, I was crushed with three others in the rear seat, and Clem beside me complained of a painful arm. On reaching the party, everyone went upstairs, and I pushed Clem into the downstairs toilet, helped him take off his jacket. This revealed a white shirt saturated with blood. On inspection, a neat stab wound was apparent between his shoulder blades!

Refusing all assistance, he sat upstairs against a wall. Finally, he insisted on drinking his half bottle of whisky before we could persuade him to re-enter the Zephyr and be taken to casualty at the Western Infirmary. A probe proved the knife had just missed his heart, and he caused so much trouble after a few sutures that he insisted on going home before the police arrived.

He lay in his nearby flat for a week, taking alcohol as a painkiller, and a student removed his sutures without him returning to a doctor.

The work seemed to become more complex each year, but somehow, I never failed an exam despite leaving halfway through and continuing my hectic social life.

The annual student rag week for charity saw many hilarious incidents. For example, the engineering students somehow managed to get an old car onto the roof of a department store in Sauchiehall Street. Also, the Mountaineering Club climbing the steep front of the St. Enoch's Station Hotel, engineering students turning all the traffic lights to red at a significant junction in the city centre, while bogus police officers escorted pretty girls across the city centre road, much to the annoyance of frustrated motorists.

Since security was laxer those days, one student managed to slip unseen onto the football pitch at Ibrox when Rangers were playing and had the ball at one point. At the same time, bemused players tried to point out to the referee that there was a stranger in Rangers colours on the field. It was several minutes before the referee stopped the game!

Every year, we attended a Rugby International at Murrayfield. We travelled in a coachload of medical and veterinary students armed with full beer crates.

After the match, the crowd marched like an army into the city centre, heading for Rose Street, the service street behind Princes Street. It was a straight street with numerous pubs, and each year we attempted to go from one end to the other in the company of Welsh, English, French or Irish companions. We woke up in our flat the following day with terrible hangovers and the opposing country's scarf around our necks.

On one hot evening after an international, unusual in wintertime, my classmate Ian Mackie was arrested beside me, just outside the door of an overcrowded Rose Street pub, being accused of drinking alcohol in a public place. He was bundled into the police car, and I asked to accompany him, and for some reason, this was allowed. We were ushered into a large Police "Tardis" in Princes Street, where a disinterested Sergeant started taking Ian's details. Suddenly he noticed me sitting on the bench behind and asked the officers what I was doing there. When told I had asked to accompany the accused, he pointed out that I still had a pint of beer in my hand, gave the poor officers a rocket for wasting police time on idiotic students, and threw us out (minus the beer).

Another Saturday in Glasgow town centre saw us end up intoxicated in the Locarno ballroom, a huge hall with a dance band and hundreds of people. I noticed some of my friends surrounding a vet student in another year, known to be on the eccentric side. The interest was caused by a starting pistol he had, which was being passed around for inspection. When my turn came, I jokingly pointed it at the ceiling and pulled the trigger, not realising it was loaded. Then, to the astonishment of all, there was an enormous bang. The band stopped dead with screaming dancers scattering everywhere. Two large bouncers grabbed me within seconds, carried me through the front door, and launched me over the pavement into Sauchiehall Street, where traffic narrowly missed me.

Fortunately, the anaesthetic effect of McEwan's beer left me with only a few bruises the following day.

I thoroughly enjoyed my student days. After the horror of dissecting dead animals at anatomy lessons and living with the smell of formaldehyde, I enjoyed pathology particularly, examining diseased body parts. (Back to my Spilsbury days!)
Physiology, biochemistry, microbiology, pharmacy and many other subjects followed, and gradually we moved towards treating live animals.

I particularly enjoyed an Easter holiday staying at the University farm to learn how to deliver lambs. I have small hands, and this was a great advantage when trying to deliver twins or triplets with a presentation in the ewe's birth canal of various legs and bits belonging to different lambs, which was great fun to sort out, then watch the babies struggle to their feet and go straight to mum for milk.

We slept on the farm and cooked in a large kitchen. One morning it was the turn for Barry Philps, a classmate who later emigrated to New Zealand, to cook a fry up for about six of us on an old cast iron gas range.

We were all sitting on the other side of the room as he fried bacon and eggs.

Unbeknown to us, he was confused by the controls. While at his culinary work, he was unaware that he had switched the gas on in the oven below. Suddenly there was a massive explosion, and we were rendered temporarily deaf.

Amazingly, Barry was lying on the floor, dazed but unhurt, even though the blast had blown the oven door clean off, and it had taken a chunk out of the ceiling before landing in the middle of the room. Presumably, the blast had blown Barry out of the way a millisecond before the door hit him, thus saving his life. It took half a day for our hearing to return!

Soon we were out at the brand-new Veterinary Hospital outside of Glasgow for the serious side of learning diagnosis and surgical procedures, with brand new operating theatres and modern equipment. Again, the staff were brilliant, and since there were only forty in our year, we had very intensive high-quality training.

One Monday morning, Dai and I were allocated a large grey Glasgow police horse with a swollen foot as our first case. Unusually for a Sunday, we had been to a party the evening before, and both of us had a hangover.

Dai elected first to hold the horse's head while I stood on the patient's side and lifted his left back leg. As I prodded his foot, he suddenly reacted in pain and hangover suffering Dai was not concentrating too well and lost control of the animal's head. The horse looked round to the site of pain, to be presented with my backside, a target he could not resist. It sank his teeth in it!

My turn to react in pain, and I had a complete set of horse teeth marking my rear for weeks and found sitting down difficult for at least a week!

Another time, one of our several day cases was a collie with a skin problem, which was our last case one morning before the lunch break. When 1 p.m. came, we had a rush to get up to the canteen before all the cheese rolls were gone. As usual, we ran up the stairs, and Dai carried on to the queue while I had a quick tiddle in the toilet on the way. A week later, I found some irritating skin lesions in a very embarrassing place and made an appointment with the University Doctor.

I told him about the skin case and that I had forgotten to wash my hands afterwards in my rush.   He ignored me and proceeded to deliver me a lecture on my morals and to prescribe some ointment. Since I had seen him early evening, I went back to the flat and applied the cream to the affected area.   Within seconds I had a terrible burning sensation, threw off my clothes and sat in a cold bath for a quarter of an hour.

On Monday, we received results showing the collie dog had Ringworm, a rare fungal skin disease in dogs, and transmissible to humans. Immediately remembering my visit to the toilet and how I had omitted hand washing, I knew what my medical problem was. The hilarious staff in the Vet Hospital Dispensary agreed to give me a human dose of Griseofulvin antifungal tablets, failing to record it in the records to spare my embarrassment. Despite their promises of secrecy, I was greeted for days by lecturers
and fellow students continually enquiring about my health with great grins on their faces.

That summer holiday, fifteen vet students from Glasgow hired three yachts on the Norfolk Broads, each with five onboard and at least one experienced sailor.

The craft had sail only, a tiny rowboat with a sail on tow, and a quanting pole in case of no wind at all. We had a hilarious week, covering a fair bit of the beautiful countryside, passed windmills, wildlife, and inevitably moored each night near a pub. I managed to get wet three times, once returning in the overloaded towed dinghy returning from a pub and once when we were becalmed.   I had a tiring spell on the quant pole, resulting in me having difficulty removing it from a river bed, and as the yacht moved on, I was left dangling from the pole till I fell in.   The third episode still terrifies me, and I still suffer occasional nightmares.

One morning the boats were moored at an inlet on Horsey Mere, a very large lake. My friends had shown me how to tack in the tiny towed dinghy behind each yacht, and as I was first awake that morning, I decided to have a try in our dinghy on my own, practising up and down the inlet, since there was sufficient wind for the small sail.

I then had a not so brilliant idea to go out into the edge of the lake.   As I passed the last yacht, the next person to show was the girlfriend of my classmate Colin Silver, the only girl present in fifteen of us.

She shouted to me that if I was going onto the lake to be careful, and as I passed, she dropped a life jacket into the boat, which I put on, and in doing so, she saved my life. However, as soon as I passed the thick row of tall reeds around the lake, the wind seemed to treble in intensity.   My sail immediately filled, and I shot off into the mass of water at a reasonable speed, in no time covering a surprising distance. I had not expected this and realised I must try to return, as I had been taught the day before.

The inevitable result saw my craft overturn, and I was not strong enough to turn the little boat back up correctly. Clinging to a ridge on the upturned boat, I realised it was early Sunday morning, and I could not see another boat on the lake.

I now realised what a situation I would have been in without the life jacket since the distance to the inlet was beyond my poor swimming abilities. I got cold within half an hour, and my fingers were numb, trying to hang on.

Fortunately, the girl Julie was now asking if the others had seen me return, and soon the two best sailors were on their way in the other two cockles to fish me out. So a cold and scared student was returned to blankets and hot tea and given a rocket by all for my stupidity.

Every student Saturday evening started with drinks in a pub, then evenings in the basement bar of the Union building. Dreadfully rude songs were sung endlessly (I remember most of the words to this day).

After closing time, we rushed upstairs to the dance hall, where a band was starting, and a line of young ladies, mostly students, or nurses, were arranged looking for the man of their dreams.

At the time, Glasgow had Strathclyde, now a university in its own right, teaching colleges, art schools, and many other places of learning, including the School of Domestic Science. In those days, no one wanted to be a chef, and most students were girls. Sadly the establishment had the unfair reputation of being for students at the lower end of the educational scale. It was known in the student world as the "Do School."

A classmate at Ayr Academy, Roddie Crooks, who always wanted to be a chemist, was now a fellow student, and one Saturday Union event asked a girl to dance. As they struck up a conversation on the dance floor, Roddie asked the girl what she was studying, and she replied that she was at the "Do School." She then asked Roddie what he was doing, and he replied that he was studying pharmacy.

The girl's eyes immediately lit up, and she exclaimed, "Oh! You're going to be a farmer!"
I don't think there was a second dance.

The Union dance floor became a cinema on Sunday evenings. 7.30 p.m. on Sunday provided great entertainment, watching on the steps outside the Union when hungover students tried to remember the appearance of a girl they had asked the previous evening to the cinema show.

The scene of many meetings and many changes by Monday, the dance floor had reverted to a copy of the House of Commons, with identical seating, and when debates were staged, a speaker's chair and replica mace.

I watched many future politicians argue there in debates, including John Smith, who later became head of the Labour party in Britain, who sadly died prematurely.

Another Shadow parliamentarian was Donald Dewar, who talked non-stop in debates. The favourite of all the female students was Liberal Menzies Campbell, who was very good looking and ran for the U.K. in the 1964 Olympics.

While I was a student, the Honorary Rectorship of Glasgow University became vacant, and the students had to vote for a new one. Unfortunately, there were only two candidates, Donald Duck, and the only other was someone we had never heard of, who was in prison in South Africa. His name was Nelson Mandela, and everyone in our flat voted for Donald Duck. Luckily Nelson Mandela did become Rector, a post he held all his life.

One of my classmates, an Irishman named Liam McNeil, was a particularly sporty type and often flew back to Ireland to play Gaelic Football and was into fishing and other country sports.

A good rider, he competed in show jumping. At one event, he was standing behind a horse when something spooked it. He received the full force of its rear hooves, landing in the pit of his stomach. An ambulance appeared, meaning that he was on the operating table at the Western Infirmary within less than sixty minutes, and a colossal incision allowed the removal of yards of his crushed small intestine, saving his life. Incredibly Liam bounced back in no time from this horrendous injury.

My classmate Alasdair was a keen sailor. His father was a doctor, and a medical research consultant, who owned a house at Tarbert harbour on Loch Fyne. I went there to stay on holiday frequently. He had purchased an old ship's lifeboat on one occasion and already had a yacht and dinghies in Tarbert harbour. So he arranged to sail it down to Helensburgh on the Clyde to have it checked out, intending to convert it into a cruiser.

We set off from Tarbert with his parents and Alasdair's attractive red-haired, younger sister Deirdre who was about fourteen at the time.

All went well till we were opposite Gourock at the entrance to the Clyde when the engine started to struggle, so we attempted to make Gourock when it packed up entirely, just short of it. But, unfortunately, efforts to restart it failed, and the anchor started to drag, with the current carrying us away from the port. We were so close but had no mobile phones or radio at the time. So we decided that Dierdre, also an experienced sailor, should row our little towed boat into the harbour. She achieved this magnificently and located an engineer who came back with her, complete with his bag of tools.

By this time, the stationary boat was wobbling in the waves, and Dr Govan, wearing all-weather gear, helped Alasdair and I lift the engineer and his kit aboard. Somehow in the process, Dr Govan managed to fall into the water. Unfortunately, due to his clothing, he had difficulty swimming, and at first, we could not seem to pull him out till the engineer suggested pushing him hard under the water. Finally, with the help of the upthrust when he reappeared, we got him safely aboard.

After that drama, the engineer identified the engine problem and managed to restart it.
We kept it running, and Dr Govan paid him.   Deirdre rowed him back ashore, and fortunately, her slim features made her easy to pull back aboard.

All this took a considerable time till we started in fading light for Helensburgh, still quite a distance on the opposite shore of the Clyde.

It was dark within a reasonably short time, and when the lifeboat lights were switched on, they did not work. We were left unseen in the middle of a busy shipping lane. A large cargo ship passed close to us very quickly, totally unaware of our presence, and her wake sent us rocking and rolling.

At least one other large ship passed close, and Mrs Govan's contribution to the crisis was lying at the bottom of the boat crying for her mother!

Eventually, we reached Helensburgh in one piece and tied up at the boatbuilder's yard.
I had previously been out on a yacht from Tarbert to Arran and encountered a very violent storm, but that was not as scary.

We still partied madly on weekends, but gradually our workload became huge. Finally, I had my 21st birthday celebration, and my friends presented me with a pewter tankard in time-honoured fashion. Later that evening, the traditional moment came when I drank a pint of beer in a oner with no hands. The tankard had a small lip on it, making it possible to grip it with my teeth, and I accomplished the feat with ease. That tankard is sitting at this moment on the bar in my lounge.   It still bears my teeth marks from the occasion.

The same challenge nearly resulted in the death of a vet student in one of the years above me. Hayden Christie lived in one of the residence halls, and my classmate Ian Mackie and other students went out to celebrate Hayden's 21st.

The moment to down the pint in one finally arrived, and some of those arranging it stupidly poured a large amount of whisky into the beer without everyone's knowledge.
Hayden polished it off, and a few moments later, collapsed on the floor.

By good luck, several were final year medical students who gave artificial respiration till an ambulance arrived. Luckily, he survived the stupidity of his friends and lived to tell the tale.   I vaguely remember that he married a fellow girl student in his year, who was very attractive. But,

82

unfortunately, her name was Jenny Taylor, and the poor soul had to put up with her unkind nickname of "Genitalia" for five years!

At the time, we lived in fear for several days at least, throughout the Cuban Crisis, and the evening it reached its peak, we decided that with the world on the brink of nuclear war, we would go to the pub to enjoy what might be our final evening. Unfortunately, due to the nuclear submarine base in Gare Lochhead nearby, Glasgow was a prime target for the Soviet Union.

Returning to the flat the worse for wear, I went to the toilet, and on returning, found my friends clustered around our ancient valve radio, which was not very reliable. They were frantically trying to relocate the B.B.C. signal and told me solemnly that they had just heard both sides had launched the missiles, and we had four minutes to live! We sat in stunned silence, counting the time on our watches, and as we got to six minutes, they started to giggle about my terror.

I was not very happy about their cruel joke, and I hope never to have to repeat the final four-minute feeling!

In the final year, most of my friends went to an annual University Union event in December. Still, I did not have a current girlfriend at the time, an unusual occurrence!

The function was called "Daft Friday" and amazingly exists to this day. It was Black-tie, with formal dinner in the restaurant. There was dancing to several bands, all sorts of activities like the sizeable cinema, snooker, table tennis, bar open all night, and breakfast at four a.m. for those still capable of standing up!

Fate intervened, and the next day in the city centre, I bumped into my school sweetheart Marie, who was studying to become a teacher in Glasgow, and engaged to another teaching student. We had rarely seen each other in the five years since school days, and she agreed to be my partner at the event, which was a great success. As a result of this agreed one-off date, my life changed dramatically, and we were soon back to our school romantic intensity.

This romance eventually led to our engagement and a final term of cramming for finals in the spring. I spent weeks at home in Ayr studying till all hours, then back to the imposing Bute Hall of the University for the final written examinations, followed by examining many sick animals, accompanied by a scary independent Professors from a neutral Universities, being grilled on our diagnosis, the whole process being terrifying as each tried to prove we knew nothing.

We attended the old college a week later with great trepidation to witness the results, traditionally pinned on a notice board. Finally, I was delirious to see that I had passed, qualified as a veterinary surgeon, and walked away from the chaos on my own, to cross town, and tell Marie.

I ventured into New City Road in a dream and was brought back to reality by the scream of brakes, to find a double-decker bus beside me and a furious driver who was screaming obscenities at me after my narrow escape! I, therefore, almost had the shortest veterinary career of all time!

Graduation day was a grand affair, and Marie and my proud dad and mum were there to enjoy it with all my happy colleagues. Before going onto the platform in the massive Bute Hall, my name was Jacobus (My first name in Latin) Watson to receive my scroll. I somehow managed to graduate with distinction and won the Clinical Medicine Medal, despite my hectic student days, which were a wonderful time of my life. However, I realised that real-life lay ahead with responsibilities!

After a short engagement, Marie and I enjoyed a church marriage in July 1965 and a brief honeymoon in England, ending with my being the best man (returning the favour of the week before) for my friend Dai who married his childhood girlfriend, Diana.

Their honeymoon in Newquay was not a success in one way. Dai, a strong swimmer, decided to hire a Malibu surfboard, and before long fell off, the board hit his face, damaging several front teeth! He spent each day of his honeymoon sitting in a dentist's chair.

Back in Ayr with my parents, I searched the Veterinary Record to find a suitable position as an assistant in practice. I quickly noticed an excellent post in North Cornwall, where I was offered a position as a junior assistant with a practice house rent-free.

I had earlier been offered a position on the medical staff of Glasgow University at a new Vet Hospital in Nairobi, where Glasgow was helping set up a new Veterinary teaching establishment but chose a career instead in practice.

At the same time, Marie, now a qualified teacher and still an amateur actress, was offered a position as an announcer for the B.B.C., which she also turned down.

Chapter Twenty-Three
Stourport-on-Severn

We moved to Stourport, and I liked Roger Vale, Eric Smith, and John Barton, the partners, with Eric doing his best to help me establish the small animal work.

The downside was that I only had one receptionist to help who was not keen on holding animals, or helping during operations, hating the sight of blood! Quickly the new premises started to attract new clients, but I was certainly thrown in at the deep end with so little help. Marie had a small boy to occupy her day, so she could only assist occasionally. Somehow, I quickly gained confidence, and the practice became busy enough to have a nurse to assist.

I still did a little farm work, and the practice was pear-shaped, extending south into the Clee Hills. Calls going far into this area meant keeping a supply of old pennies in the car since before driving 10 miles back, we had to find one of the ubiquitous red phone boxes and use four pennies to check with the base that there were no new calls in the area. No cell phones in those days!

The area towards the village of Cleoberry Mortimer was frequently cut off by snow in winter. The practice owned an old Land Rover, which carried tyre chains for work in the wintertime in that area.

One Christmas Day that I was on call, the local doctor's surgery called asking if we had anyone on duty calling near Cleobury Mortimer. I had several calls, and one was to see a very ill cow right there. So I called in at the local G.P. practice and was given two village addresses and a loaded syringe.

On the way in, with the Land Rover ploughing through a foot of deep snow, you always passed a memorial at the roadside to a postman who had perished there many years ago. He had attempted the journey in a blizzard. Not too reassuring. We always carried a flask and blankets when going to that area.

On this occasion, I saw the cow, then called on an old gentleman who had pneumonia. I gave him the antibiotic injection from the doctor's surgery and, with some trepidation, visited a lady who had given birth that morning. Fortunately, she already had three children, and her husband had delivered the baby successfully. Mother and baby seemed fine, so I was relieved.

In another instance, I visited a Hereford bull with an abscess on a swollen foot. The animal was impossible to handle and clever enough not to head into any crush restraint. Finally, the farmer and helpers enticed him into a communicating passageway using cow nuts as bait. As he ate, the plan was to hang over a wall on one side and plunge an antibiotic into his substantial rear end.

The farmer and helper clung to my waist as I dangled above the patient. I was terrified they would lose their grip, in which case I would have been doomed.

After the fourth and last day on that Saturday morning, I felt very relieved. The final call that day was to a sick budgie that managed to bite me. I emerged from the house to find a traffic warden giving me a ticket. He asked me why I was bleeding all over the pavement, and I told him what had happened. He laughed at my reply and let me off my parking error.

Winter farm visits were challenging in the snow on icy roads. On one occasion, I was in my Hillman Hunter when I came to a long steep hill on a minor road. I started a dreadful skid on applying the brakes, gaining speed towards a left-angled bend at the bottom.

Straight ahead on the corner was a gate into a field that was open. My speed made it impossible to carry the bend, so with my hand on the horn, I went straight into the field of snow and attempted to keep the car moving. Incredibly I saw another open gate at the end of the field where I sailed back onto the road again.

Near Stourport was a monastery, where one day I had to visit some lambs and trim the feet of several donkeys which the monks kept.

The very last donkey was extremely wild, and Father Peter and Father James had great difficulty holding it, wearing their cassocks, and bare feet with sandals. At one point, it lunged so much that I lost the leg that I was holding, enabling the donkey to free itself enough to deliver a smart kick which was a direct hit on Father Peter's shin. I was shocked to hear the worst outbursts of obscenities as he hopped around in agony!

Another winter day, I left Stourport in a blizzard and spotted a monk walking beside the road in sandals and bare feet in a foot of snow, carrying a large holdall two miles from the monastery. Recognising him, I stopped and told him I would drop him home. I insisted and, opening my boot, lifted his heavy bag into the car boot with difficulty.

As I drove on to the monastery, I asked what was in the bag, and the reply was 48 jars of marmalade!

Although I did mostly small animal work, I still did some large animal calls at weekends on call. For example, on one of the main routes out of Stourport was a long straight road that crossed a piece of flat scrubland stretching for nearly a mile. One Saturday, I received a call at midnight from the local police asking me to attend an animal accident.

Every year, I knew that Romany gipsies appeared, parking several caravans on one side of the main road, and I hoped that it did not involve one of their ponies, which were usually present amongst the vans.

The scene was chaotic, with several police cars and an ambulance, all with flashing lights. I could see a red Mini with a smashed windscreen

86

and several bloodied youngsters being loaded into the ambulance, looking very shocked.

My patient was a small Shetland pony that had been on a chain, and whoever tethered him did not notice he had enough spare chain to cross the road to find some better grass.

The Mini, full of youngsters, was travelling fast and hit the chain, propelling the pony into the air, with it landing on the bonnet, and its head went through the windscreen.   Several of the youngsters had facial injuries, but none seriously hurt.

The Ambulance departed, the police cleaned up the broken glass on the road, and I was surrounded in the dark by several gipsies carrying oil lamps, who led me to my patient.

The pony seemed incredibly well; he could walk, but his nose was plastered in blood, and he was making funny noises breathing.

To my surprise, they lifted the pony inside a caravan with his head facing the entrance, and with the aid of lamps and torches, I cleaned up his head and nose and discovered that the only injury was a huge slice that had almost severed the end of his nose.

The gipsies talked to the little fellow as I injected local anaesthetic into the area of his nose, partly hanging off to one side.   As I waited for this to take effect, I looked around in the dim oil light at all manner of China plates and decorations hanging from the inside walls, very neatly stacked. Then, as my eyes grew accustomed to the poor light, I looked above and was astonished to see a toothless grin from an old lady with silver hair in the bed above me in a rack, on one side, watching me operate with a grandstand view! I was concerned about keeping the patient's nostrils patent and finally took the plastic inserts from two large bands of sticky elastic tape.

My helpers boiled them in water with my surgical instruments, and I carefully sutured the nose, including the inserts, to keep the breathing space clear and prevent the sides from adhering to each other. Finally, after an anti-tetanus and antibiotic injection, I announced that I had done my best but could not guarantee success.

"Will you still be here in a couple of days so that I can come back and check him?" I enquired.

"We'll stay as long as it takes to get 'Arry right!   That be a fine job you 'ave done, and we be so grateful since 'Arry be the children's favourite, so we 'ave to get 'im well.   Thank 'ee from all of us!"

Stepping back out of the van, I suddenly became aware of a bunch of small children who must have watched the whole episode, and each came forward, shook my hand, and said, "Thank 'ee Sir."

After I had packed my gear, I found a crowd of swarthy adult men around me. The one with the lantern said, "Ow much, Sir?" and I watched the faces around me with trepidation.

"T..Ten pounds, please," I stammered.

"Excellent young 'un," said the leader and produced from his pocket an enormous wad of notes. I had never seen so many in my life!

"Here be twenty pounds for your boss and ten for yourself," he announced. So I blew the ten pounds on taking Marie to the Areley Hill Hotel, and we toasted 'Arry in Château Neuf de Pape!

Several times I called in to check 'Arry, and by the time I had removed the sutures and implants, Harry was none the worse for his accident. I appeared to be a hero to the small smiling children surrounding me.

Stourport was quite a pretty little place, especially near the river, where a fledgling industry began. The town was connected to canals, which years before had been so crucial for the transport of coal and manufactured goods throughout the Midlands in the heyday of barge travel. Now, some enterprising locals had realised the possibilities of tourism in hiring barges for canal holidays, and many freshly painted barges were appearing for the purpose.

The drive to Bewdley along the Severn River was beautiful, and there we had a minor branch surgery for dogs and cats, which I usually took, transporting surgical cases back to the Stourport premises.

One day, I called to see a Jack Russell dog with a sore foot and ended up at a small mid terraced house, where a kindly elderly gentleman opened the door.

He was very tall and smartly dressed in a pinstriped suit and waistcoat. He showed me his little West Highland Terrier, who was licking his foot. I could see a swelling on top of the foot, which often meant a grass seed had penetrated the area. I learned that he took his walk in a nearby park every day, where he loved to run around in the long grass.

As the client held the little fellow in his arms, I noticed something protruding from the swelling, which appeared to have just burst. Using a pair of artery forceps, I grasped the object's tip and gently pulled a grass awn from the wound.

"That should do the trick!" I announced, telling the grateful client that his pet was very well behaved since usually, removal required a general anaesthetic. He was very appreciative and told me his wife had died years ago, and the little dog was his only companion.

I accepted the offer of a cup of tea, and while he was in the kitchen, I noticed a glass cabinet in the corner of the small room. Inside were several caps and medals, and when he returned with the tea, I enquired about them.

"These are F.A. Cup medals and my England caps", was the reply. He then went to the fireplace and grasped a photograph partly hidden by a jar, handing it to me. "That is the King presenting the F.A. Cup to me at Wembley."

I was astonished and learned his name was Jesse Pennington, and he had played centre back for West Bromwich Albion and captained England for several years. He was very lonely, and I had a fascinating half-hour with him and offered to check the dog in a week.

The little dog had made a good recovery, and if ever I was near his house on a quiet round, I used to call in for tea. He was an incredibly kind and modest man, sadly very lonely. I often wondered if any of his neighbours even knew what a famous resident lived in the street, who had played at The Hawthorns every second week to enormous crowds, then worked as a plumber during the week. How times have changed, and I considered it a privilege to have known him.

The waiting room at Areley Kings soon became bustling, as there was no appointments system those days. One day the receptionist told me my next patient was a Newfoundland dog named Winston, and I ignored her grin. Instead, I opened the door to the waiting room and saw a huge black and white dog on the other side.

Barely in the room, I shouted, "You are next, Winston!"

He bounded across the floor, leapt up with his forelegs on my chest, and in a second, I was flat on my back as he stood above me, licking my face! The others in the waiting room were in hysterics of laughter, in an image straight from the current T.V. series, where a similar fate regularly befell Fred Flintstone. So the next time I saw Winston, I made sure I was better prepared!

Marie was now expecting a second child. Having just delivered piglets, I arrived just in time at the Lucy Baldwin Maternity Hospital for the birth of my first beautiful daughter. (Lucy Baldwin had been the wife of local M.P. Stanley Baldwin, who was Prime Minister in the thirties, presided over the affair of King Edward and Mrs Simpson, resulting in the abdication).

After days of indecision over the baby's name, Marie suggested Imogen, a name unfamiliar to me. We agreed, and I later found out that the name originated as the Italian Innocencia, which in England became Innocence and then Innogen.

In one of Shakespeare's plays, Cymbeline, a character was Innogen. Unfortunately, when the printer prepared the letters, he was unfamiliar with the name and mistakenly read it as Imogen, which went onto the manuscript and was published. I have read it is the only U.K. name to owe its present state to a printer's error.

Although it took some getting used to, it ended up the perfect name for my beautiful daughter, Imogen Jane.

By this time, I felt that my future was in small animals only, and I longed to be working in an environment with other vets specialising in that field. Although I worked with friendly partners and immensely enjoyed Worcestershire, they understood the direction I wanted to follow.

Just after I left Stourport, partner Eric Smith, who had been very kind and helpful to me, died suddenly with a massive heart attack, and his widow Pam kept in touch with us.

Not long afterwards, the practice suffered another blow. In his late thirties, partner John Barton was kicked in the face by a horse, suffering a completely smashed jaw and substantial dental work, and had massive surgery to repair his jaw. After a lengthy recovery, he amazingly decided he had lost his confidence, went back to studying, and qualified as an optician.

Eric's son Martin had been a teenager when I was at Stourport and had an emergency appendectomy. I visited him in hospital two days later and told him a joke. He laughed so much that his sutures came apart, his wound herniated, and he had to be taken back to the Operating Theatre to have it repaired. His mother Pam then banned me from revisiting him!

Although I enjoyed Stourport and doing more small animal work, I realised that I would prefer to see only domestic pets. To do so would mean yet another move in a short time. Still, Marie understood how I felt. So the Vet Record came back under scrutiny, resulting in a successful interview at Rickmansworth, where the older of two partners in a small animal practice wished to retire in a year or so.

Chapter Twenty-Four
Rickmansworth

Rickmansworth was now my third job in four years, and I hoped that things would work out. However, though Marie always agreed with me when we discussed the future, I felt that moving house might eventually test her patience.

We moved into the practice house, which was called The Old Vicarage, and was a lovely spacious old property on the main road at Croxley Green. It had a lovely open space opposite, with two pubs situated on it, a fact which I noted immediately, among expensive houses in a beautiful setting.

The practice was on the other side of town on the main road out to nearby Uxbridge and started long ago by Pat Cousins and her husband. Sadly, after a short time, he had run off with a client, and she had divorced him and carried the practice on in his absence.

Eventually, Colin Thomas had joined her and became a partner, and she was thinking towards retirement, needing an assistant who might replace her in a year or so, which was precisely my plan.

Pat still did some Equine work, and there were a few farm clients, but 95% was pet animals.

I had never anticipated working with anyone like Pat! She was short, attractive, with dyed platinum blonde long hair, and bubbled with personality. She was an excellent surgeon and quickly helped me improve in that regime. For a change, this time with the proper equipment and plenty of nurses to help. The building was well-equipped and added to, extending back with each extension further into a vast garden.

The downside of working for Pat was her explosive nature. She once told me she did not consider she had done her job correctly if she did not make all the nurses cry at least once a day. At first, I was astonished at how the staff took her, screaming at them so frequently about errors or mishaps. But, the rest of the time, she was so friendly and kind that everyone tolerated her outbursts. She even brought me near to tears once or twice, but I put up with it as she was invariably correct, and I became a fast learner.

She was not opposed to shouting at clients, and one day I saw her at the exit door onto the pavement of Uxbridge Road. A client she had refused to see again was standing at the open door on the pavement with a cat in a basket.

Pat was shouting, "Go away! I won't see you again!" and the protesting client kept lifting the basket into the hallway, asking forgiveness, and Pat kept lifting the basket back outside! Unfortunately, I never found out the outcome or story.

Colin was a kind, gentle vet, and very interested in tests and the clinical side, and happy for me to concentrate on surgical cases.

One particular story I will never forget, as one that should never happen. Colonel Livesey was living on an upmarket housing estate across the main Uxbridge Road. He was a retired Army officer who had several Siamese cats, one of whom was brought in to have some teeth out. With usually two vets operating all morning, the urgent cases were operated on first, and more routine ones later on.

Several times during the morning, the receptionist came in saying Colonel Livesey was asking if his cat was ready to collect. Pat and I were both operating at different tables in the large theatre, and each enquiry was answered by Pat saying we had not got to the cat yet.

Just before lunch, as the end of a busy session was near, the receptionist appeared again, saying, "Colonel Livesey was on the phone again."

There came a typical statement from Pat. "Tell him that we have not done his bloody cat yet!"

There was a stunned silence when the receptionist entered again and said, "He wants to know why the cat is sitting on his lap and still seems to have her bad teeth!"

Houdini came to mind when we realised that not only had the cat escaped from a pen, but must have exited the kennel room, gone through the preparation room, through the x-ray room, through the waiting room, past reception, out of the front door, and crossed the busy main Uxbridge Road to find its way home.

As soon as Pat had finished her operation, she took off her gown and walked to Colonel Livesey's home. In her unique way, she managed to appease him and returned with the cat. She removed the teeth and took the cat home, which was quite a feat.

She then returned to the operating theatre calling all the staff in and screaming abuse about the incompetence of everyone in not noticing the cat's miraculous journey. I suspect Colonel Livesey was not charged! But, as usual, it was the fault of everyone but her.

Amazingly, as life went on, I grew to like her despite the odd outburst and rapidly learned to emulate her fantastic skills.

Since we were close to the Uxbridge Road Film Studios, we had a few celebrity clients. Although there was no appointment system in those days, certain well-known clients were always given one.

Pat still did some equine work since she rode to hounds and was well up in that circle.

One client with ponies was Muriel Pavlow, who lived nearby and starred with Kenneth Moore in "Reach for the Sky," the film about Douglas Bader, and Dirk Bogart in the Doctor films. I told Pat that as a teenager, I had Muriel Pavlow's picture on my bedroom wall while I was at school but sadly never managed to accompany her on her occasional pony visits.

Sometimes I knew who was in the waiting room, always crowded, when I heard continual laughter. This meant the presence of a Boxer dog owned by the famous comedian Jimmy Tarbuck.

He was always polite and modest in the consulting room and very kind. However, when I suggested he could have an appointment, he always refused, saying the situation in the waiting room had given him ideas for jokes.

One day, I answered a local police call to attend an address at a house in town. Arriving, I was told that a middle-aged lady who lived there and had not been seen for days. On breaking down the door, the police could see a large German Shepherd facing them at the end of the hall, and they had asked for a vet to attend and go in first to deal with the animal.

I armed myself with a choke lead, and as usual in such circumstances, arranged my large case carrying all my drugs in front of me as protection. I asked the tallest officer to draw his truncheon and follow me in, telling him that if the dog charged us, hit it on the head (Don't tell the R.S.P.C.A.!).

I spoke kindly to the dog, which seemed interested and attempted to stand, but immediately collapsed again. I could smell gas, so I shouted over my shoulder, "Gas! **Do not touch** any light switches!"

I slipped the lead over the poor dog, who wagged his tail feebly and feeling the dehydrated skin on his neck, I could tell he had drunk no water for many days. Then, leaving the dog, the officer and I peeped into the living room, where a worse smell was evident. Flies buzzed over the woman's body lying on the floor. She had been an alcoholic, and the room was full of empty spirit bottles. Broken glass was on the floor. It looked to me as if she had fallen and severed an artery in her ankle and was so drunk she had bled to death.

I was glad to get some fresh air outside and suggested to the officer in charge that re-homing the dog would be very difficult, as the neighbours knew it had been with her for many years. I took the responsibility to euthanise the poor dog as a humane decision, and an upset officer assisted me.

Another strange visit was a call to a house to see a sick monkey. In the sixties, the laws were not strict regarding keeping wild animals, and I went to a townhouse. Entering the lounge, I immediately noticed that the furniture was in a poor state. Again, the monkey was the culprit, probably acting out of boredom.

The creature was relatively small and looking very sorry for himself, sitting on the floor puffing away. As the owner, an elderly gentleman held him, I listened to the monkey's chest, diagnosing pneumonia. Then, giving a poor outlook, I filled a plastic syringe with antibiotics and asked the owner to pin the monkey's arms.

The second the needle penetrated his arm, there was a loud crash, and for a few seconds, we could not understand what had happened.

I had forgotten how dextrous monkeys are with their feet, and he had used his foot to grab the syringe from my hand and throw it on the floor. Fortunately, we were by now using plastic ones, and with the wife holding the little monkey's feet, the treatment was given. Unfortunately, as I predicted, the poor little fellow died that evening, and I felt it was a welcome release from cruel imprisonment.

Driving home, I remembered my former employer, Boss Harvey, narrating when he was called to Bertram Mills Circus visiting Newquay. One of the patients he saw that day was a large monkey with an abscess on his bottom, which Mr Harvey decided to lance. But, of course, he had more sense than me and had plenty of helpers to pin the patient down. But, just as he was poised with the scalpel blade, he became aware of two large eyes staring at him from a few inches away, as the monkey was supple enough to bend down staring between his legs despite the attentions of the handlers. So, he watched his minor op.

The main event was to castrate a zebra, which took place in the big top ring. Mr Harvey approached the trainer and explained that they would cast the zebra to the ground (with the ropes he was carrying), as they did with horses and place a mask with chloroform over his head. The trainer announced that the ropes were not needed, whispered in the zebra's ear, and the patient lay down on his side, much to Mr Harvey's amazement. Then, as the chloroform was administered, the trainer again whispered to the zebra, who remained quite still, and went happily under anaesthetic for the surgery.

Chorleywood Green, near me, was where Barbara Woodhouse, the T.V. dog training expert, lived, and Pat Cousins made visits there to see her many dogs. One day Pat was elsewhere, and I had to make a call instead.

Mrs Woodhouse was displeased that Pat was away for a few days and tried to diagnose the problem and suggest several days of treatment. Since she was reasonably accurate, I went along with the course of injections. By the end of the week, the dog was better, and she was happy that *she* had been correct about the treatment.

I suspected that her secret way with animals might have had something to do with the fact that she seemed to wear long woollen skirts covered in dog hairs. This way of dressing seemed to give her a great attraction to dogs. I was glad that I did not have to do any more visits.

Not far away lived Val Doonican, and my only visit to his aged German Shepherd was not a happy one. The poor dog had collapsed, and I explained quietly that there was no treatment I could give. We had a long conversation, and I was able to peacefully end the lovely dog's life with dignity as Val held her, sobbing quietly. So I left the sad household of a famous person who could not have been kinder or more grateful.

At the end of the surgeries garden was a little shed, and I found that this was the assistant's surgery every Friday at 3 p.m. I was shocked to learn that there was a mink farm near Rickmansworth. The mink were fed fishmeal, and every week several were brought in, always with the same problem. The owners would enter the mink pens wearing equipment like a beekeeper and use thick gloves to catch the sick patients.

They were put into crush cages and arrived in the shed, which smelled awful from the previous week. (The smell was from their highly developed anal glands).   Using the crush cage to pin them down, I injected barbiturate anaesthetic into their abdomens, and slowly they absorbed the drug and went off to sleep.

The problem then showed as a considerable abscess swelling in the neck.   On lancing this, a search with forceps produced a large fish bone, which had penetrated the oesophagus. This bone was removed, and a drainage hole was left open, which, when released, left a healthy mink to one day be part of a rich person's coat.

The Old Vicarage was a lovely house with woods behind and some other excellent properties nearby. In those days, my collie cross Tim did I admit, wander off on weekends, searching for discarded fish and chips from the Saturday night revellers.

One sweltering August Sunday morning, I watched from my lounge window as he appeared in through the front of the garden with a large complete roast beef tied up with string in his mouth. I ran outside, but he was faster than me and shot off into the large wood behind, returning in the late evening looking very happy.

I heard no more about the incident but can only imagine one of my neighbours had just taken the roast from the oven and placed it on a unit near an open back door.   No hue and cry followed, and I did not usually speak to or see any of them, but a few days later, I looked into the garden to see Tim straining on the lawn.

"I don't believe it!   He has a colossal tapeworm!" I shouted and went to investigate him with a tissue in my hand. I grasped the end of what I now realised was a string and slowly pulled it out in its entirety.   The string had been around the stolen roast beef.   Tim was back to his routine the next day.

At the time, my practice vehicle was a mini estate.   One weekend I had taken John, now a lively three-year-old, out somewhere, and Tim was also in the back seat of the car.

I had to return home for something I had forgotten and parked briefly in the large driveway.   I shot into the house to retrieve my wallet from my jacket. Suddenly, I heard my car engine start-up, and as I looked out of the window, it started to move forward with John steering. He held the steering wheel while standing on the driver's seat, with Tim standing on the back seat wagging his tail! (No child seats those days!). By the time I ran outside, the car had traversed a straight line for about 15 yards and impacted the six-foot garden fence separating the front of the house from the back garden.

I had only erected it a few months before to make John safer while playing in the back garden! The car stalled, the fence was pushed back at 45 degrees, and the driver was unhurt and laughing after the adventure. As it was winter, I had left the choke out and the car in gear instead of applying the hand brake, and worst of all, left the keys in the ignition. I found it hard to believe that the car had moved without the clutch operating or that John had known how to turn the ignition key. Finally, after a dressing down from Marie, the panic was over.

Chapter Twenty-Five
Stately Home

Rickmansworth had some very wealthy clients, and one day, I heard Pat and Colin arguing about a large amount of money outstanding from a famous client who owned horses, dogs, and cats. Pat refused to take them to court for the amount owed, and Colin insisted this should be done.

I only did one visit to the house, situated on a large estate with a security gate. I had been told what to expect and was interviewed by the guard before nervously
proceeding up to the mansion.

It was a practice rule always to wear a suit and tie on visits, and I rang the doorbell. As I expected, a uniformed butler opened the door, and I explained the reason for my presence. However, I was asked to wait in the large hall as he disappeared with my visiting card on a silver tray.

As I gazed at beautiful pictures on the wall, he reappeared, handed my card back, lifted my bag, and announced that Lady .... would see me now. He then knocked on the lounge door, opened it, and stood in the doorway with me at his side. "Mr Watson, the Veeeeterinary Surgeon," he boomed, carrying my bag towards the lady, who was holding a long-haired Persian cat.

Fortunately, the cat was friendly and only required the removal of sutures after being spayed. This was achieved, and the lady was very nice to me, and I decided not to mention the outstanding bill. She then rang a bell; the butler reappeared and carried my bag out to the car. As I drove away, I wondered how many other local firms she owed money to. "Butcher, baker, candlestick maker......?"

One Friday evening, I was on duty. I saw a friendly little pug who was in labour and making no progress, so I ended up performing a successful caesarean resulting in six lovely live puppies successfully delivered after midnight.

That Saturday morning, I was on duty on my own, and as usual, the waiting room was packed full at nine a.m. Opening the door for my first client was to prove the worst moment of my career!

At the insistence of all in the room, the lady owning the pug was first in the queue, carrying the mother and newborn puppies in a basket. The mother was lying there very quietly as the puppies squirmed about in small intestine. Unfortunately, the mother had chewed out all her sutures, which resulted in the wound herniating and abdominal contents everywhere - my worst nightmare with both partners out in a waiting room full of patients!

Within a minute, the mother was anaesthetised, and on the anaesthetic machine, and a drip in place. The pups were happy on a clean Vetbed in the basket while I cleaned up all the intestines in a warm antiseptic fluid.

97

Then, I replaced them and syringed out the abdomen before closing it again. I was happy that my experience with poorer anaesthetics had taught me to operate very quickly, and the whole procedure was accomplished in twenty minutes. I was pleased to announce to the horrified clients in the waiting room that all was well, and the pug and babies would all be right as rain. Thankfully I never had to repeat the experience, and the Pug and puppies recovered well.

The practice had a small branch in Watford, which Colin had started up, and it was equipped for routine operations. The building was called The Old Bakery, and unlike the primary practice, accepted cash only for treatment.

There was a local Greyhound track, and many Greyhounds were seen, some owned by rather dodgy clients, which Colin had learned the hard way!

When Colin was on holiday not long after I started, I ran the Watford end when he was away. I enjoyed the change from the chaos at the Rickmansworth end. The nurse helping me was a bright, red-haired, attractive young girl called Alison, who, while I was at Rickmansworth, became one of the first qualified Veterinary Nurses in the country.

Alison and her husband Tony became good friends of Marie and me, as we found that living in Rickmansworth was very different to what I was used to regarding social lives.

Marie and I were restricted socially with two young children, but I found the local pace of life near London very different. A few Saturdays that I was off duty, I ventured to the two local pubs on the green opposite, talked to some lovely people, and then did not recognise a single person on my next visit. I played a few cricket games for Rickmansworth, and again every week seemed to be different players. Every time I spoke to someone I liked, I found they had moved to the other side of London or a similar story at the next game.

My student friend Dai now lived in Chandlers Ford and had joined Round Table. On his recommendation, I managed to go to a function of Chorley Wood Round Table. Unfortunately, I found that all of the members seemed to be wealthy business and professional men, and I felt entirely out of my depth financially, so Round Table disappeared out of sight for the moment.

After a year, the only social friends we had were Tony and Alison, and I was being sounded out about the partnership situation, which had suddenly changed dramatically.

For the first time since her first husband's desertion many years ago, Pat had met a lively Irishman who was very interested in racehorses like her. He had a great sense of humour, and it was evident that the situation was changing rapidly, making Marie and I do a bit of soul searching about the future.

Pat did most of the Equine work, and a call came in when she was away when a couple came in to arrange the castration of two ponies. They explained they were gipsies, and they would have to take me to the site. I quoted them a fee and told them they would have to pay cash on the day, to which they agreed. Since Pat was not around, and they assured me the ponies were docile, I decided to do the surgery that afternoon since the weather was fine. I, therefore, set off after lunch following their very ramshackle car to where the ponies were waiting.

We seemed to go a great distance and ended in a field, almost at the end of Heathrow Airport, with aircraft flying very low overhead. A couple of large Romany caravans, children playing, and two enormous cobs were standing close by in the field. "I thought you said they were ponies!" I exclaimed.

"Well, they are quite strong," was the reply in an Irish accent.

"Do you have the money?" I enquired in a not very professional manner, sizing up the situation.

"Right here, Sir," was the reply, as he showed me a large bundle of notes.

I arranged all my sterile instruments and selected a patch of long grass for the procedure. The couple were to assist, and another fellow was also around.

The owner told me he had never had a pony castrated before, so I explained that I would inject an anaesthetic into the jugular vein in the neck. In about ten seconds, the pony would collapse on the grass.

Since the pony was so large, I made sure those holding knew which side I wanted it to fall, if anything, to make sure none of them was underneath. Then, with hot water and a rope and all my equipment ready, the owner and wife held his head, and the other helper stood by to help push the pony onto the side I suggested.

They talked to the pony, and he kept quite still as I entered the vein and gave a hefty dose of Thiopentone. The pony wobbled within a few seconds, then crashed to the ground, exhaling a massive loud breath as it landed heavily. "Bee Jasus, you've killed him!" shouted the owner.

"He's fine," I replied, quickly roping a hind leg and giving it to the helper to pull away, exposing the pony's scrotum. I cleaned and washed the area with antiseptic in no time, working at top speed to commence the operation. By this time, I thanked the good Lord that the pony was breathing again and completed the procedure in about five minutes while the owner still panicked beside me.

Very relieved, I waited, and within ten minutes, my patient was starting to recover, and within fifteen minutes was standing up supported by the owners. "By God, you were right! Now I know what to expect next time!" the owner yelled out.

The second pony was very quiet, fortunately being very used to being handled, and within an hour, all the work was completed.

99

I enjoyed a cup of tea as I waited to check for any bleeding, and all the time, airliners noisily went overhead on take-off or final approach. They were so low; I could make out the rivets on them and see the pilot's faces!

The happy owner paid my fee, and I did not tell him that was the first time I had done the operation without another vet accompanying me!

Work in the practice was hectic, and I was rapidly becoming more confident in surgery, especially as Pat seemed to do less due to her new friend. Then, one day I was presented with a white Standard Poodle with a large umbilical hernia. Many puppies have small ones at birth, and as the pup grows, the hernia usually closes around a ball of fat sealing the abdomen.

This one was full of small intestine, making surgery advisable. Unfortunately, Pat was away for the day, so I elected to operate that afternoon. I was shocked to find intestines in the hernia and a pair of artery forceps.

The nurses confirmed that Pat had spayed the bitch a few months before, and though the surgery was simple to correct, I was panicking about telling the owner! So finally, I contacted Pat by phone, and she suggested telling the owner that internal stitches had given way and not charging the owner for the operation.

Pat told me to impress the staff that any mention of what had happened would mean instant dismissal. Though my instinct was to tell the truth and not charge the owner, I had to go along with the story.

We certainly had some unusual clients, and none more so than Miss Brown, who lived in a large house, alone apart from a servant, and had a very unfriendly, obese, aged Cocker Spaniel named Peter, who was Peter the Third.

Several times I had to visit him to administer monthly steroid injections for arthritis.
Fortunately, Peter was so fat; he could not turn and bite me when he had his treatment.

Miss Brown was knowledgeable and told me her father (now deceased) had been a director of a sizeable British aircraft firm, whose name I will not mention, as it still exists. She was still on the board of directors.

She was in her late fifties and usually offered me tea. One day when she left the room to arrange my tea, I was looking out of the window when I noticed a pile of aircraft drawings on the table beside me. "Top Secret" was stamped at the top of the page!

Sadly, a short time later, Peter deteriorated with age, and Pat euthanised him. We then had a phone call saying she wanted him cremated, as a pet crematorium had just started in Kent, so we arranged for his remains to be collected.

The longest-serving nurse at Rickmansworth was Mike, unusual those days as a male assistant. One of his jobs was drug ordering, and he was always complaining to me about Colin meeting drug representatives and ordering all sorts of new drugs to try, usually to the annoyance of Pat, who was not so keen to pay for them.

We had an exciting phone call from Miss Brown to say that the crematorium had posted the ashes of Peter Brown to the practice, yet she had not heard from us.

Enquiries I led failed to locate them, and the last person I spoke to was Mike, whom I knew usually dealt with the post. He was sure the ashes had not arrived yet, but after a moment said, "Hang on a minute, I've just thought of something!"

I followed him into the consulting room, and he walked up to the enormous shelves of drugs, stopping at the section for stomach ailments. He reached up and lifted down a large white plastic container.

He told me he thought this was some new drug Colin had ordered from a rep and meant to ask him about it. He thought it looked like a charcoal type powder for tummy trouble.

There was nothing written on the container, and I opened it to see grey powder, and on closer inspection, small pieces of bone! "Good Grief! It's Peter Brown!" I exclaimed.

Indeed there must have been a letter with it. A sheepish Mike said all he remembered was a mass of tissue paper round, it so there could have been a letter inside that he threw out accidentally. "By the way, I knew nothing about the cremation!"

Since the occasion had caused a lot of interest in the practice, I found that hard to believe. I was relieved that Peter had not been prescribed to a patient with diarrhoea.

We contacted the crematorium without telling Miss Brown, and they apologised that his name was not on the container.

The container was duly delivered and buried by the gardener. A few days later, Miss Brown telephoned to tell us she was delighted and asked if it could have Peter numbers one and two exhumed and similarly cremated. We managed to convince her that was not a good idea.

Towards the end of our stay in Rickmansworth, my sister Alison and husband John came to live in nearby Amersham since John's firm had placed him to work in the London office for a time. Usually, his occupation took him worldwide, and it was good to have them nearby for a while.

I loved being near London with my interest in cricket, which John shared, and we spent a few visits to Lords to watch Middlesex. I also loved visiting the art galleries and was astonished when the Hayward gallery managed to arrange an exhibition of most of Van Gogh's greatest paintings from all over the world. I attended a day off midweek and was astounded to find a quiet day where I could get close to many of my favourite paintings and even touch them, a unique chance that will never be repeated due to the risk and insurance.

I considered the visit a great privilege, and in years to come made two-weekend visits to Amsterdam, where I visited the Van Gogh Museum. As well as many paintings I had already seen, there were many I had not, not to mention thousands of his letters to his brother Theo and even brushes and palettes he had used.

I remember staring at "The Yellow House," where Gaugin and Van Gogh lived in Arles Provence and stood there with tears rolling down my cheeks!

Later that year, my parents came down to stay for a week as we had not seen them for some time, and they were able to spend time with John and Imogen. Sadly, I did not know that this would be the only time my mother would hold Imogen in her arms.

Pat, by now, was convinced she wanted to retire. Colin hoped I would take over as his partner. However, Marie and I felt that Rickmansworth was too close to London, and this was brought home on summer weekends with good weather.

Local parks were jammed up with people, and the nearest seaside was at the end of a massive traffic jam. Having both spent our childhoods in Ayr, a seaside resort, then Cornwall, which we both loved, we wondered about trying to return to the West Country.

Pat and Colin were very disappointed with my decision, but Pat reluctantly accepted that she would have to work for longer until she found a vet to succeed.

I saw an advert for a position in practice on the edge of Truro, and they were looking for a vet interested in small animal work. So I arranged an interview. They had premises in mind in Falmouth and needed a vet with small animal experience to develop it. They assured me that anyone making a success of the venture would become a partner.

A similar situation to Stourport but in a beautiful part of the West Country, and Falmouth on the sea! I liked the partners, who were impressed by my experience and desire to return West. I liked the look of Falmouth and was immediately offered the position.

We spent a convivial evening together, and I telephoned Marie, who was delighted to return to the West Country. I stayed overnight with the senior partner, and all the pleased partners came for breakfast.

The telephone rang as we were tucking in the following day to a typical English breakfast, and the vet on duty looked glum. Then, finally, the senior partner's wife came into the room and surprised us all by saying, "It's for you, Graham."

I picked up the phone in the hallway. It was Marie, who told me that Alison had just left, having broken the news that my mother Kit had died suddenly in Ayr, and Alison's husband John had booked us all on a flight to Glasgow in two days. I was shocked since she was a lively 67 years old and went back into the room badly shaken.

After some thought, I told the partners, who were keen for me to start as soon as possible, that they had better forget me and look for someone else in the circumstances. They told me I could contact them if I wanted to reconsider since I was the candidate they wanted.

Chapter Twenty-Six
Canada

All my life, I would think of my student experiences and some of the ridiculous episodes during my university summer holidays, and the most interesting was my visit to Canada and the U.S.A.

In the summer of 1963, my classmate Alasdair and I decided to spend two months visiting Canada, resulting in two veterinary students in kilts hitchhiking around the country.

We started our journey taking off from Prestwick Airport in a D.C.7., four-engine propeller-driven plane, making a scary initiation into the flight. This trip was courtesy of Caledonian Airways, which had just started the business after buying three outdated aircraft. On take-off, the plane shook and rattled, while unnerving flames shot out of the engines, as we agonisingly slowly gained speed down the longest runway in Britain, till we struggled into the air due to the weight of fuel carried. Then, slowly we gained height over the Firth of Clyde, with both of us panicking if we would clear the Island of Arran, which loomed closer.

Fortunately, we did, and darkness soon closed in, and as it was a night flight, passengers nodded off to sleep. However, I was so excited I could not sleep, and having been offered the chance to go to the cockpit, I ended up staying there for most of the journey. Fortunately, there was no headwind or else we would have had to refuel at Gander in Newfoundland. Just in case, our flight took us over Newfoundland, which, apart from the coastline, appeared like a never-ending stretch of rocks as I imagined the surface of the moon might be! We landed in Montreal, and on the freeway, joined a group of students trying to hitch a lift to Toronto.

Soon two cars stopped, ignored all the other candidates, and both drivers came up to the two lads in kilts, and a heated exchange began as to which driver had seen us first!

Eventually, one gave in, and astonishingly the winning driver revealed he was a veterinarian in Toronto.

He dropped us at a new car delivery firm whose address we had acquired at home.

They asked us to deliver a brand-new Nash Rambler Station Wagon to Vancouver, which for us hit the jackpot! After providing all our documents, he gave us a quick instruction on the controls and pointed out an automatic gearbox.

Untruthfully, I told him we were experienced with that, and we got into the car parked in front of the gas pumps. I started up, somehow selected reverse in error, and we shot back across the fuel area, narrowly missing a poor lady filling up her vehicle.

The dealer ran back in a panic, and I had difficulty convincing him that my foot had slipped, and I knew what I was doing! Eventually, we slid into the rush hour traffic, driving an automatic for the first time and on the opposite side of the road!

The journey through Toronto city centre was a nightmare, but eventually, we were on our way. Still wearing our kilts, we stopped at a cafe for a bite to eat, causing consternation with our attire.

A couple from Hamilton who had Scottish ancestors approached and asked us to divert and stay with them for the evening, as the next day was Hamilton Scottish Highland Games. I had never attended one, but Alasdair was a reasonable bagpipe player and soon played a borrowed set to our host great glee, ensuring a few days more stay at a luxury house with a swimming pool.

Three days later, we left there in our brand-new station wagon and swam in Lake Superior before undressing in the heat and climbing into sleeping bags in the spacious rear of the vehicle. The windows were open and the interior lights on, and, unknown to us, admitted half of the local mosquito population. Lights out and exhausted, we looked forward to a good night's sleep, and instead, within minutes had mosquitoes buzzing in our ears, and in despair, Alasdair leapt into the front, opened all the windows, and we drove off at speed, with the driver stark naked. Fortunately, no police were around, and we learned a lesson about lights and open windows!

Soon we were driving over the prairies and wheat fields with hundreds of miles of never changing wheat, finding out the hard way how hungry the local deer flies were every time we made a stop. Finally, we called in at Calgary at the address of one of my father's cricket friends who had emigrated a few years ago. That evening they drove us north to an inland lake, and in the late evening, we had a fantastic view of the Aurora Borealis.

We drove over the superb Rockies, marvelling at the change from the flat prairies with the long straight Trans-Canada Highway, which was a three-lane road with little traffic in those days. At least twice, I had to remind Alasdair he was driving on the wrong side of the road, which was easy to do in these circumstances.

Eventually, we reached Vancouver, and I knocked on the door of my Aunt Connie, who had emigrated in 1917, as the wife of a Canadian soldier fighting in the First World war. She had crossed the Atlantic on the Olympic, one of the sister ships of the Titanic. I still have her diary of the voyage in lousy weather, with the ship zigzagging to avoid German submarines.

My Aunt spoke with an English accent still, after all these years with Uncle Horace, a quiet man who had fought in the great Canadian triumph at the Battle of Vimy Ridge in 1917. He was a friendly man, and it was challenging to think of him fighting hand to hand in the trenches.

Their daughter, my cousin Grace, lived with her husband in a large house nearby, and we stayed there for a few days. She started life as a singer on TV, then joined a bank, becoming Canada's first female bank manager. She was an attractive blond and was also extremely clever.

I was less impressed by her husband, who was very large and seemed to be a permanent university student. He showed us the basement of the large house, which had a replica English Pub at one end for parties, and the rest of the long space was a shooting gallery.

He showed us his gun collection, which went from a Winchester rifle to a Tommy gun.

We were astounded when he told us he had these to use when the Russians came! Like many Americans at the time of the Cold War, he was sure Armageddon was coming soon.

The next day, he took us to his gun club and handed me a vintage Colt 45 (the favourite cowboy film gun). I had never fired a real gun before and though not very keen, tried a few shots. Next, he handed me a German Luger brought back by a G.I. from WW2, which he had purchased.

I took aim, pulled the trigger, and the fierce recoil sent me flat on my back to his great amusement and that of the audience nearby, who were expecting it.

As our trip was nearing our end, I was glad to set off on the journey back to Toronto.

Amazingly, and I have never understood why, a new British Mini that had been delivered to a gentleman in Vancouver who now wanted it driven in a hurry to Toronto.

This suited us fine, as Alasdair and I could share the driving while he slept in the back!

He was not impressed when I had difficulty starting it since finding the starter button on the floor took time.

After 1500 miles, we pointed out it was due for a service, so our benefactor told us to pull into a garage.

Much hilarity was caused since it was soon apparent that the car was too small to go on a ramp, and no tools fitted it. In the end, we topped up the oil and left to cheers from an astonished bunch of mechanics! We made the trip in 4 days by alternately driving through the night and sleeping in the passenger seat.

Our employer was delighted, and we arrived shattered but early for our flight home to Prestwick.

When safely home to my relieved parents, I glossed over the scary bits of the trip, such as our trip to the Okanagan valley.

The friendly people who gave us a lift to Penticton found us some work fruit picking locally, and the first day was a disaster. I spent all day picking cherries, ate too many, and spent a sleepless night with intense stomach pains. I have not faced a cherry since.

Soon a chance came to go fire watching in the valleys of the foothills of the Rockies.

We opted for a two-week shift, and forty of us went to the hills in a coach, with around twenty students and twenty American Indians.

One tent for the food and a blanket was our night-time bed since it was scorching. The following day, I woke to cries and banging noises and watched the foreman chase four black bears from the food tent, where they were banging maple syrup tins together, showing they were experienced thieves.

Later in the week, Alasdair and I sat on a hill above a valley, and forest fires were burning not far away. On the third day, the valley below was smouldering, and then to our amazement, flames appeared at the far end of it. In a short time, wild animals were racing away from the fire, and sadly many were not fast enough. As arranged, we used our walkie talkie, as we called it, to report to base. We retreated to the next hill and watched as planes came in low to drop foam while others dug windbreaks further on.

The whole business was terrifying, as we realised humans could suffer the same fate as the animals. That evening there was a rain shower, and everyone cut some branches from the fir trees to make an improvised shelter in case of rain at night. There was no more rain, but when I woke, I was horrified to find I could not open my eyes.

The foreman immediately pointed out my forehead and eyes were massively swollen, and he told me it was a spider bite from the branches above my head, and if I lay still, I would be fine by lunchtime.

His medical advice was spot on, and I enjoyed the campfire meals with my colleagues.

After the first week, we were surprised when the coach took all the young Indians away for the weekend. The foreman explained they had been paid and would all be drunk all weekend in town. They would all return on Monday except those arrested for fighting, and 19 returned on Monday. I soon learned that sadly, many of the indigenous population who had been driven from their lands so cruelly had failed to adapt to the twentieth century and were a deprived section of the community.

Chapter Twenty-Seven
Yeovil

I was very disappointed at Rickmansworth, feeling that everything seemed to be against me, and three positions in four years was not an excellent record. However, after the sad visit to Scotland for my mother's funeral, I recommenced my search for a West country position. An interview at Honiton was not suitable, but I was offered an interview in the Yeovil and Sherborne practice a week later.

The interview produced an opportunity similar to the Rickmansworth one. The Yeovil senior partner wanted to retire to the country, having already moved there, and the Sherborne partners were more interested in equine and farm practice. However, one of them did the Sherborne small animal work.

Robert Brown, the senior partner, whom I liked on first meeting, was Scottish and had done mostly large animal work and did an evening surgery at his big house in Yeovil, where we would live. He had recently moved to a nearby village, as he prepared to retire, and he felt that someone was needed to build up the small animal work. Although the other practice in the town centre did some small animals, both partners were older men not interested in that side. However, I was still expected to help with large animal work, which I did not mind.

Moving into the large house with a waiting room, consulting come operating room, and some recovery pens, I felt I could immediately start a morning surgery. The old front garden was already a large car park, and behind the Victorian house, there was a large field with plenty of space for expansion.

The innovation of morning surgery time, Saturday morning, and long evening hours quickly began to attract a significant increase in clients. Each day I did routine operations with Marie helping me at the start. After some time, I engaged a girl to help part-time as work built up.

Although I was not back in Cornwall, Yeovil was a good-sized town, Sherborne was pleasant, the surrounding countryside was beautiful with pretty villages, and Charmouth and the coast 40 minutes away. I still did some farm work and enjoyed these visits to the area around Yeovil and Sherborne.

I received one call to a young bullock that the farmer had caught in the field and tied to a gate with a halter. The animal was a fair size and had a very painful eye with a heavy septic discharge.

A helper pinned him to the gate, and his owner held the patient's nose as I attempted an examination. Infectious conjunctivitis was pretty typical, which the farmers called New Forest Disease. This problem was always seen in both eyes.

I tried with difficulty to clean it up and thought I could see a possible foreign body.

Finding a pair of artery forceps in my bag, I managed to grab the black object, and at the crucial moment, the beast gave a lunge away from me in objection to my efforts. As it did so, I was left clutching the forceps with a large piece of barbed wire attached. I rechecked the eye. I could see nothing more, and I applied antibiotic eye ointment and gave an antibiotic injection since daily treatment was impracticable. The patient was by now opening the eye almost perfectly and already feeling very much better. I left a happy farmer and patient and felt pleased with my effort.

Another spectacular case was a lame cow, which had recently calved and been in a loose box beside the muddy yard near the farmhouse. On examination, it was unlike any lame cow I had seen before, with a hugely swollen foot and a standard leg above. I cleaned it up and at the end of the swelling was an indentation. It was almost as if someone had applied a tourniquet.

We managed to get it in a crush for closer examination, but the indentation was so swollen I had difficulty seeing into it. So, finally, I took a scalpel and tried to push it into the indentation, where I could now touch something hard. The poor cow objected in pain as I experimented with the scalpel, till suddenly there was a pinging sound, and something started to come away. I found myself holding a bloody black length of rubber, and the farmer exclaimed, "It's a rubber ring from one of my wife's homemade jam jars!"

I gave the cow antibiotic by injection and visited two days later, the leg was incredibly back to normal, and the cow was walking fine. So I repeated the injection, declared the case closed and walked away with several jars of homemade strawberry jam!

Chapter Twenty-Eight
Charlotte

Soon after this, Marie was admitted to Yeovil District Hospital Maternity Unit. I managed between calls to be present at the birth of our third child, the lovely Charlotte Mary Catherine, and our family was complete.

Later in the year, I attended a calving that was to prove unlike any other. On arrival, the farmer told me it was a bizarre one, which he could not understand. On examination, I could feel legs, no head but definitely what felt like intestines. I told the farmer it must somehow be a calf with a burst abdomen, and I could not seem to exteriorise any of it. However, a caesarean operation could save the cow for breeding next year, even though we both knew the calf would be delivered dead.

Since the cow was young, the farmer agreed. He would rather have a good heifer and one that was a good milker. As usual, I cleaned the site with the cow tied in a stall, gave an epidural and local anaesthetic, and proceeded to open the uterus.

I was presented with a nightmare scenario. Body parts, a head which I could not free, and legs all mixed up. Somehow the object seemed almost square! I could not find any way of finding a presentation that would come through my standard incision size. I stopped for a moment and explained that the only way to deliver it was to enlarge the incision into the uterus and body wall if that was possible.

The farmer observed that we had nothing to lose as he would lose the cow unless the calf was removed.

I anaesthetised a larger area at both ends of the incision and waited for a while before scrubbing up again for another attempt. Eventually, I pulled the calf out through a massive incision and immediately realised it was completely deformed. The animal was shaped in a circle, with the back of its head attached to its tail region. As it lay on the floor beside us, its internal organs were exteriorised and with no covering. Incredibly the heart was beating, but the lungs could not inflate, and intestines spilt around the heart. A pretty dreadful sight, and the poor farmer was vomiting a few feet away.

I concentrated on closing the uterus, then the muscles and skin of the cow's enormous incision, accompanied now by a pale-faced farmer. The cow stood happily eating hay throughout this operation, disinterested in all the chaos, my anaesthetic having worked well. She recovered quickly and had a regular calf the following year.

Returning home, I researched and realised the calf was a rare deformity where the original circular embryo does not separate. As a result, the head remains attached to the end of the spine, making it impossible for the usual coverings of the chest and abdomen to develop. The chances of my few years in large animal work turning up a deformity

like this were infinitesimally small.   The condition is known as
Schistosoma Reflexus.

Yeovil was a pleasant market town, and the large house above the
practice premises was delightful. Next door was the large British Legion
which I quickly joined, and I was delighted that they had live music.

Many years before, when I was a student, it was customary on
Saturday nights for student parties to take place in flats near the
University Union after closing time.   If you brought some beer and knew
someone, you stood a chance of entry.

Sometimes a student would turn up carrying a guitar, and they would
always gain entry.

This musical aspect prompted me to purchase an old acoustic guitar from
a junk shop. Though I could not play it, it did get me entry to parties,
usually in packed chaotic flats where none could remember who brought
the guitar, but someone present could usually play enough for a drunken
singsong. Of course, I then made sure to take it home later.

My classmate Clem taught me a few chords, and I used to practice in rare
moments over the years.

Saturdays, Marie usually elected to stay in with the children, and I
would pop next door to listen to bands in the Legion. Sometimes when on
call and we were both in on Saturday, Marie would threaten to ring next
door to complain about the noise, as Imogen's bedroom was on the side
of the house near the Legion.   I never dreamed that I would be in a band
making the noise there in a few years.

The opening of daytime surgeries soon seemed to get around the
"bush telegraph," and work started to build up quite rapidly. At that time,
Yeovil had a population of around 35,000 and a catchment area of
villages nearby. Westland Helicopters, Pittard's glove makers, and the
weekly market, along with the Fleet Air Arm headquarters at Yeovilton,
near Ilchester, only 5 miles away, were the leading employers.

At the time, Westlands employed six thousand people and was very
important to the town. I was told that a few years before, Prince Philip
visited the large establishment and made a tour of the helicopter
assembly lines.   He walked up to an older employee, and enquired "How
many men work in here?" After a short pause, the reply was, "I reckon
about half of them, Sir."

Chapter Twenty-Nine
What's the Time?

One day I was presented with a Yorkshire Terrier, vomiting after swallowing a child's watch. An x-ray revealed the watch was lodged not in the small intestine, the usual presentation, but the oesophagus.

I knew surgery in this situation was complicated and decided to refer the case to the University of Bristol Vet School at Lower Langford. The next day, they rang me to say that they were going to operate, and they had noticed that since the child's watch was a luminous one, a great feature those days, several x-rays had shown the watch still keeping time!

The head surgeon removed the watch, but sadly the oesophageal wound broke down, and the little patient did not recover.

At the time, there was a greyhound track in Yeovil, and I had been warned about prescribing sedatives for "barking Greyhounds annoying neighbours." The tablets could be given on the night for racing dogs to affect performance since there was no drug testing those days.

An early morning call came in from a Greyhound owner who had a large number of racing dogs near Yeovil. He told me that two stud dogs had got into a pen of bitches and young dogs, where a bitch was in season, and there had been a massive fight. Incredibly one young dog was dead, and several dogs had been bitten in the melee, one young dog having a severe throat gash. The stud males had survived with wounds, but a fight like a Wild West Bar in a cowboy film had ensued. Fortunately, I managed to repair the youngster, but I will never forget the incident.

A very nice lady, married to a local doctor, was an enthusiastic breeder of very friendly Golden Retrievers. She telephoned to say a new litter of puppies were suddenly unwell.

I arrived in the nearby village, and the house had a large garden with a purpose-built shed for whelping cases, which was heated and very clean. The bitch lay in a corner on blankets, and the puppies were all around, looking unwell and vomiting. I looked at one puppy's eyes, thought I detected a slight yellow tinge and told the owner I suspected Leptospira Icterohaemoragica infection.

I asked her to remove the mother and puppies and borrowed her husband's tool kit from her house. I set about the false floor of the shed with a chisel, and as I removed it, I exposed a rat's nest full of baby rats and a mother who abandoned them and shot across the lawn!

Although the dog's mother had been vaccinated against this disease as a puppy, she had received no booster injections since. As it is a dead vaccine, the mother's immunity had fallen and given no protection to her puppies.

Luckily, the owner had quickly realised that they were ill, and suitable antibiotic injections to mother and babies resulted in all surviving, as irreversible liver damage had not had time to take place. I left further antibiotics for her doctor husband to give each day, and all the pups recovered. However, the owner was so horrified that she decided to keep further whelping bitches indoors.

Since the Fleet Air Arm headquarters was at Ilchester five miles away, I had many clients and friends in the service over the years. Not long after I arrived in Yeovil, I drove past a large new roundabout beside Yeovil Hospital, and police stopped the traffic. Almost immediately, a military helicopter landed on the roundabout. I later learned that a Westland Gannet anti-submarine plane from Yeovilton had crashed nearby. Sadly, the pilot taken to hospital in the helicopter did not survive.

Over the years, I became familiar with many aircraft, including famous Westland helicopters like the Sea King, Lynx, Wildcat, and Merlin, flying overhead.

Many fixed-wing aircraft operated from Yeovilton throughout the years, including Hunters, Sea Vixens, Buccaneers, Phantoms and Harriers.

I was already familiar with the Buccaneer since I was still in Cornwall during the Torrey Canyon oil tanker catastrophe. Little was known then about tackling the situation, and some bright spark came up with bombing the tanker to destroy the problem. This tactic, of course, only made the situation worse, but I well remember the Buccaneers coming low over St. Columb, performing victory rolls on their way to land at St Mawgan on the return journey.

At one time, when the Hawker Hunters were used there as training aircraft at Yeovilton, I was quietly offered an unofficial trip in a two-seater trainer version by a contact at the base. This event was suddenly cancelled when a trainer Hunter had an engine failure. Two people were safely ejected before the aircraft crashed in a nearby field, fortunately without any human or animal around. Unfortunately, the passenger turned out to be a civilian not supposed to be there, and that was the end of my chance of a flight!

The person, luckier than me, had a flight in a jet fighter and a parachute jump thrown in free, along with membership of the Ejection Tie Club for aircrew who have successfully fired an ejection seat.

At the time, the Phantom aircraft were at Yeovilton. I went to a Round Table talk given by an American pilot who had served in Vietnam. He was instructing Fleet Air Arm pilots on the Phantom. Afterwards, I enjoyed his company, and he asked me to come out one evening to look around his place of work. He asked about my family and suggested I bring John, aged about twelve, with me. He met us at the gate, and showed us around the Phantom simulator, and allowed John to sit in it for a demonstration.

He had organised the evening perfectly, and took us out in the dark onto the edge of the runway near the Control Tower, pointed to two Phantoms lining up together for take-off, and explained it was a night interception exercise.

The ground shook as they passed us at great speed, seeming to go straight up with the bright red of the afterburners giving a fabulous display in a clear night sky. We then walked swiftly up the Control Tower steps, where he showed us on a large radar screen that they were already over Bristol and flying in excess of Mach one.

It was two days before the annual Yeovilton Air Day, and we went into the Officers mess for a drink. On the opposite side of the bar was a fresh-faced young man in an R.A.F uniform drinking an orange juice, making me think he was under eighteen. However, when I pointed him out to my American friend, I received the reply that the lad was the pilot for the Lightning solo display in two days, and he had just arrived!

It has never failed to astonish me with the variety of different cases that a vet may face. An excellent example was a call from a middle-aged client who was a landlady of a Yeovil pub. She explained that her cat was expecting kittens, and for several days had insisted on sleeping in the corner of a wardrobe in her bedroom on a pile of clothes that was about to go in the washing machine. This morning she had discovered the cat in situ, with three very active newborn kittens. All seemed well, but later in the morning, a problem had occurred, and she needed an urgent appointment.

The lady quickly appeared and brought a basket into the consulting room complete with cat and kittens. She told me she was very embarrassed, but there was a big problem with the kittens.

I managed to remove kittens only from the basket and was astonished to find them entangled in an item of clothing: a pair of frilly knickers. The kittens had been struggling, with their tiny claws all tangled in holes in the many perforations in the item. Trying to disentangle them seemed impossible. So, in the end, with the owner holding them, I painstakingly used forceps and sharp scissors and slowly snipped around each kitten till it was free, then carefully trimmed away till each foot was free of material. Incredibly, this took a quarter of an hour, and with the squirming, squeaking kittens upsetting their mother, she had to be removed from the room. Finally, all was well, and a happy, if embarrassed, owner left with the new family, determined to make a suitable bed in the wardrobe.

By now, Marie and I were starting to make friends in Yeovil in several ways. I had started to play cricket for Yeovil, and as an opening batsman, scored a couple of fifties in my first two games for the second eleven.

The following weekend I was off duty and told I was selected to play for the first team at Dean Park, Bournemouth, the Hampshire County ground. This was the old ground before the new ground outside Southampton, which now stages test matches. I was amazed when shown the local paper, where the back sports page had a banner headline saying, "Vet steps in for Yeovil." This build-up did not help my confidence when I arrived at the large pavilion at the County Ground. Yeovil elected to bat first, and I was asked to pad up to open the batting.

One of my teammates called Vic Thrower, asked if I would like him to bowl a few practice balls outside the pavilion. Accepting his offer, I made the mistake of standing in front of one end of the pavilion. The seats contained several older gentlemen wearing county ties, sitting with a white wooden fence between us, eyeing me with curiosity.

In all previous occasions of such warm-ups, I had received a few "trundlers" to feel bat on the ball, but instead of that, Vic bowled a pretty fast ball at me, which I did not expect. But, unfortunately, it passed me before I reacted and smashed a hole in the fence to the annoyance of the said members!

I did not know that Vic sometimes opened the bowling for Somerset Second Eleven, and after retreating clear of the fence, I wandered sheepishly back into the dressing room.
Scoring only 10, I made my sad way back into the pavilion, and as I passed the home members, walking back up the steps was sure I heard "Idiot!" muttered as I passed by.

I played for Yeovil eventually till age 45 years, mainly in the second XI partly due to difficulties playing away games. I was also the club chairman for many happy years.

During one summer in holiday times, I was asked to captain a Sunday second eleven away at Dorchester. We struggled for a side, and I was offered a father and thirteen-year-old son to make up the team.

Les Botham's father was in the Fleet Air Arm at Yeovilton, and his son was Ian. Dorchester batted, and young Ian Botham had his bowling sent round the ground. He batted number four and, after a few wild swings, was out cheaply. His father, Les, scored fifty not out and won the game for us. I tried to persuade Les to play again while we were in the bar, and I told him that I was not impressed by his son. But, as Ian went on to be one of England's most famous players, how wrong can you be, and is now Lord Botham after his charity work.

Knowing him did make test match tickets more available, and I could claim that my friendship at Ayr with Michael Denness meant that I could boast of having played in club cricket with *two* England captains!

Yeovil played in the Somerset League at that time, which meant games at Taunton's county ground. So one sunny day, I opened with friend Steve White at the county ground, which was a big thrill for us. Within an hour, we had a partnership of 100, and I had scored 60 with two sixes. I then attempted a third, and I was caught one-handed by a fantastic leap by the boundary fielder. My friend Steve went on to a century, and I still play golf with him to this day.

In the end, I became club Chairman and enjoyed my Saturdays immensely at the cricket ground playing when work allowed it, while our children played happily with their friends, children of my teammates. I had also joined the local Round Table, giving another new circle of friends, and with a friendly pub, the Somerset Inn, a few yards away, life was looking good.

Early in my new position one Saturday morning, I had finished morning surgery and a few farm calls. Since I was off duty, and it was a sunny lunchtime, I called into the Somerset Inn for the first time, hot and thirsty.

I was caught off guard when the landlord asked if I would like a cider, so I agreed to his recommendation as he poured a pint from a wooden barrel at the back of the bar.

Looking around, I noticed a none too friendly parrot squawking from his cage and hoped he would stay healthy.

After chatting with the landlord and a couple of locals (though I usually drank beer or wine), I decided to have a second pint of cider. After this, I left into the bright sunshine and arrived home feeling very intoxicated. Finally, I fell asleep in a chair despite the attentions of my children and slightly annoyed wife. Since then, I have never touched cider again, learning the hard way.

Soon the practice allowed me to employ a nurse, which was just as well, as more and more clients appeared. Then, finally, a chance conversation with a farmer's wife, while I was talking to a donkey at a gate, and awaiting the farmer to come in from the field, revealed it had belonged to their daughter, now grown up and moved away. They were looking for a new home for Coco.

Back home, I discussed it with Marie, and within days the farmer delivered him into the field behind my house, which was large enough to provide plenty of grass.

Robert Brown occasionally kept a couple of calves, and there was a stout large shed ideal for winter shelter, water trough, and an ideal situation. For a year, the children fed and looked after Coco, but he was a young male, and although not unfriendly, had started to nip a little, discouraging the children. Eventually, I started to get persistent telephone complaints from a lady in the street behind the field, saying his dawn braying was waking her baby.

I was surprised, as I thought country sounds were preferable to constant noise from low flying Westland helicopters.

We did have a donkey farm at a nearby village, so I had a word with the owner, who agreed he might be interested, depending on the donkey's confirmation. A few days later, he was mightily impressed by Coco and offered to take him as a stud donkey. When I told him I wanted no money for Coco, he was delighted, as I was with the thought of Coco and his new life with a harem.

An elderly lady client arrived one morning in great distress and told me she had been visiting friends in a village. On re-joining the A30 to return to

Yeovil, she had been involved in a collision by pulling into the path of a car coming from Yeovil to Sherborne.

She was severely shaken, and the occupants of the other car were unhurt. Her terrified Cocker Spaniel escaped from the vehicle, and she had managed to get his lead on. She tied him to the car's back bumper while she admitted responsibility and exchanged insurance details with the other party, who agreed not to call the police. They drove off, and though very shaken up by the incident, she moved very slowly for half a mile into Yeovil before pulling into a layby on Babylon Hill as a result of other cars tooting and pointing at her vehicle.

She was expecting to find some part of the car hanging off; she instead found her dog panting furiously and lying in a heap, still tied to the rear bumper by his lead. She drove straight to my surgery, and I carried the poor dog onto my consulting table. The pads on his feet were virtually worn entirely away and bleeding, but otherwise, he seemed unhurt. After a drink of water, the dog started to improve by the minute from his awful experience. I gently cleaned his feet with an antiseptic wash and lightly bandaged them before giving an antibiotic injection with tablets to prevent infection. Amazingly, Teddie slowly grew new pads with no problem over the next few weeks and months and made a complete recovery. The client failed to get over the incident so quickly. It never ceased to amaze me how so many animals seem to recover so soon from trauma.

As time went on, the client base at the Yeovil end became busier and busier, as I was now the only vet in Yeovil offering open morning and evening surgeries, and in those days did many home visits.

One day I visited a cat belonging to a local schoolmaster whom I knew since he lived close by, and we had talked in the Somerset Inn pub. The only treatment needed was a vaccination booster, but my friend had asked me to see the enormous black and white long hair do his party trick.

I quickly popped in his booster injection without difficulty, and we retired to the dining room, where a table tennis net was erected. My friend picked up a bat and table tennis ball, and the cat immediately jumped onto the other side of the table, positioned centrally.
I was amazed as the two then played a game, with the cat expertly leaping into position and using his paws to return the ball over the net every single time. Nowadays, a smartphone recording of the incident would have gone viral!

Eventually, after more than a year, my day of morning surgeries and the surgical operations, followed by visits, was taking me right through to the evening surgery, and I was finding it difficult to fit in any farm visits. However, I still took my share of out of hours farm emergencies.

One morning at 6 a.m. I had a call to say a cow had almost collapsed in a field with milk fever and was in a bad way, staggering around in a field. The farm was about 3 miles away on the A30 to Sherborne, which would

117

usually have taken five minutes' drive. However, the farm entrance was on a dip in the road, and sometimes early morning mist was a problem in that area. That morning there was an absolute pea-souper, and the short journey took about twenty minutes.

Mr Sirl was in a complete panic when I arrived and led me to the field where visibility was only a couple of yards. There was not a poorly cow anywhere to be seen where it had been staggering, and its new position could have been anywhere in the field. We spent a further ten minutes searching till a cry came from his wife, and we slowly homed in on the noise right beside a hedge in one corner of the field.

The cow was by now on her side with stiff legs and her calf beside her. Quickly I introduced intravenous calcium into her large mammary vein, beautifully exposed as she lay motionless. By the time a second bottle was given subcutaneously, the cow was sitting up and soon wobbling to her feet, having been less than an hour from death. Mr Sirl was now very happy, and by the time I returned to my car, the mist was starting to lift.

I slowly drove back to Yeovil, and just before entering the town, I passed Yeovil Golf Club, where decades later, in my retirement, I would curse that same mist preventing me from teeing off!

On one Friday, I was very excited since we had the day off, and that evening was due to drive my Morris 1000 Traveller, an estate car, to Ayr for a holiday staying at Culzean Castle a few miles from Ayr, my hometown in Scotland. My car was being serviced at a garage in Sherborne that day, and we spent the day packing, with three excited children trying to help.
As well as the service, I asked them to check the back estate sideways, opening doors, which were difficult to lock. I did not want them coming open on a motorway, with three children in danger of falling out. Then, at lunchtime, I picked the car up from the garage with all the service done.

Charlotte, just a toddler, was showing signs of car sickness at a young age, and at 4 p.m., Marie remembered that we had no travel sickness tablets. Those days the shops closed at 5 p.m., so I drove to a pharmacist in town, and it was 4.45 p.m. by the time I parked outside.

As I went through the doorway, I stepped on a set of three keys on a ring, and picking them up, found the pharmacist in an empty shop, obviously starting to clear up at the end of the day.

"Has anyone just left?" I asked, "Since I have just found a set of keys at the door, which could be for a car."

The pharmacist replied no one had been in the shop for ten minutes, and she was just about to close till Monday. So I left armed with the tablets and imagined a shopper about to find they had lost the keys to their car. So, instead, I drove to Yeovil Police Station and saw a friendly constable who booked them into lost property.

On returning home, I started packing the car, since the idea was to set off the late evening and drive to Scotland overnight when the traffic was less. Then, with the rear seats in the down position, the children could sleep in sleeping bags in the back.

I found that now I could not open the back doors of the estate at all and telephoned the garage in Sherborne telling them that I had asked for them to be checked. To my horror, they replied that a new lock had been fitted, and three new keys were added to my keyring!

I drove back down to the Police Station, and by now, it was 6 p.m., and the shift had changed. I told the officer that I had come to claim a set of lost car keys. He asked how I knew they had been handed in, so I had to explain that I had handed them in myself as lost property about an hour ago.

He was baffled by this, and he returned with a sergeant and repeated the ridiculous events of the last hour, and it took some time before they believed the story. They then explained that the officer with the lost property safe key had just gone off duty and home with the key in his pocket. While I thought about my holiday plans in tatters, the constable volunteered that the officer in question sometimes on a Friday played snooker in the Police Social Club upstairs, so went off to look for him. He was upstairs, and the key was finally brought down, and the safe opened.

As I filled in more forms, the Sergeant told me that he would only return the keys after the trouble I had caused if I donated to the Police Widows Fund, holding the collection box in his hand. All I had in my wallet was a twenty-pound note, which was a lot of money in those days, and was to see us to Scotland.

"That is your bad luck," said the sergeant, realising his sudden position of power, and only handed the keys over when the note went into the box.

On return, the keys opened the car rear doors, and Marie was not impressed to be relieved of all the cash she had in her purse to buy fuel on the journey.

We had a brilliant week at Culzean Castle, a national trust property a few miles from Ayr. The old stable yard had been converted into flats, and a Royal Artillery charity owned one for members disabled in war. Marie's father, Douglas was a lovely quiet man, had been a Physical Training Instructor. Despite his nature, he was an Army boxing champion. He had contracted malaria and bronchiectasis due to his long service in Burma fighting the Japanese and coping with the mosquitoes and monsoon seasons.

After the war, he was the landlord of a successful pub in Ayr, till retiring as his health worsened. The flat became vacant, and he duly applied, thinking many applicants would be more disabled than he was. Amazingly he was the only applicant, and Marie's parents lived happily there for many years.

119

The building was on a sheer cliff edge with only a yard to the edge. I laughed at my mother-in-law insisting on curtains in the bathroom in case someone in a boat had a telescope.

Douglas had landed a little part-time job as a guide in the castle. Since after the second world war, the grateful people of Scotland had gifted the best suite in the place to General, then President, Eisenhower, there were many visitors from the U.S.A. One evening at tea, Douglas told us that he had taken an American couple round and received an enormous tip of five pounds. He thought they were in films but did not hear their name, but he remembered the gentleman had amiable and piercing blue eyes.

The next day, Marie was upset when she found that Paul Newman and his actress wife, Joanne Woodward, had been the visitors. Her father had forgotten to tell her earlier when he came home for a coffee break, and they were still in the building at that time!

Charlotte was now about three years old, and one day I took her shopping to Sherborne, where there was an up-market delicatessen in the main street.

I went in with Charlotte and found only one customer in the shop, Lady Wingfield Digby, whose Shetland ponies regularly tried to kick me to pieces. "Hello Mr Watson, how are you?" she said.

"Very well, my Lady," I replied, hoping my greeting was correct.

At this moment, Charlotte retreated to the door and shouted in a rather broad Somerset accent, "Let's go, Dad, it's smelly in 'eeere!" I was so embarrassed by her English that we made a hasty retreat.

At around this time, Britain was in a state of mild panic. Then, for many decades, the first case of rabies in Britain was diagnosed in a dog imported from Germany.

T.V. news bulletins were full of the story for weeks at the time. Then, the next day, a new client appeared from an address I recognised as Army housing in Yeovil, which still had a small presence at one end of the town.

The dog was a Cocker Spaniel and came in with awful mouth discomfort and excess drooling and had bitten the owner when he tried to look in its mouth. I admitted the dog and carefully anaesthetised him, revealing a carnassial tooth abscess. I removed the tooth and gave antibiotics.

When the owner returned, I decided to question him more closely and with some difficulty as his English was not perfect. I somewhat panicked when he revealed that although he was in the British Army, his mother was German, and his father an Englishman who had served in Germany for many years.

To make matters worse, he told me that he was now a chef in the British Army, served in Germany, and had only come to Yeovil England a month before, bringing his family and the dog. I explained that with this history, and the current Rabies situation, I would have to keep the Spaniel in till I contacted the Ministry of Agriculture.

On telephoning the Ministry, I was informed that they would attend as soon as possible and contact Yeovil Police to send an officer to my premises. In the meantime, no other animals were allowed into my kennel area where the dog was. They would also contact the owner's employers. Within a short time, a police officer appeared who seemed terrified of the situation.

In due course, Ministry vets arrived, followed by the dog's owner, accompanied by several soldiers and the Camp Commanding Officer in a military vehicle.

He confirmed to the Ministry vets that the dog had indeed arrived from Germany, where there had been a recent case of rabies. I explained to the Ministry vets that I had been sure the dog had a carnassial tooth abscess explaining its salivation, and I had already removed the tooth.

They criticised me for not contacting them immediately and sent the owner off to arrange a course of anti-Rabies injections following his bite. They then asked me to take a blood sample from the dog, which must remain with me for the moment. So the practice activity had to cease immediately, and the staff monitored.

The Ministry vets peeped through the door while my nurse held the dog, and I took the blood sample. Then, while the Ministry vets were outside the front door filling in endless forms, for the first time, two workmen, who had spent the last week painting the side of the house, unnoticed by anyone, quietly waved to me, and I went over and spoke to them.

"Mr Watson, first we had the police here, then the Ministry vets, then the Army! What is going on?" I told them to take the rest of the day off, and I could say no more at the moment.

Within a couple of days, the blood sample was negative, and life returned to normal; and fortunately, the media did not get hold of the story. However, I was warned that I must contact the Ministry first in any doubtful situation next time, and I learned another lesson!

After just over a year of the most challenging work in my career, I began to look at my situation. I kept detailed financial books of the small animal side at Yeovil. I realised that the gross monthly turnover was already at a stage for the turnover of a one vet small animal practice, having started at very little at all when I had commenced work, only a year before.

Every month this increase was being maintained, and new client numbers rapidly increased all the time. Finally, after eighteen months, I asked if I could be included at the end of the following practice meeting, which I believe caused a bit of a stir, with some at the Sherborne leading end of the practice predicting I was about to leave for another post.

Asked into the room at the end of the meeting by the three partners, they seemed very curious about my plans.

I presented my figures to them, which showed my predictions for the future. I predicted that within a year, at least another part-time vet would be needed at the Yeovil end of the practice to assist me in pet work only. I also mentioned that I was finding that I was still being given a small farm round, which was not helping the small animal expansion at Yeovil. I was, however, still willing to help with farm work at weekends and evenings.

I also felt that the prospects of growth in the small animal side of the practice in Yeovil showed an excellent future for further expansion in the town, and I would be happy to be part of it.

With that in mind, I wondered what my chances of a future partnership were? If that was not possible, whether my salary, which was not great, could be improved by some bonus scheme, based on the increase in net profit in Yeovil. However, I did not consider this an unreasonable request considering the meteoric rise in turnover.

My comments were met with, at first, a stunned silence, and my good predictions were ignored. Instead, one partner observed that he thought I was paid well, and he had to wait for many years before becoming a partner.

None of them seemed to like my observations that the small animal side would grow significantly in years to come, and there was not a kind word about my successful increase in the Yeovil profits.

Finally, the youngest partner of the three, who seemed to show a glimmer of interest in my progress at Yeovil, asked me what I would suggest for the future at Yeovil if I did become a partner. Bearing in mind what had happened with the explosion of pet work at Stourport when the new premises was built, I gave that as an example of the progress that would probably be achieved. I said that I would plan to knock down the large house where I lived. Then, together with the car park and field behind, sell it for new housing development. These actions would enable purpose-built new premises to be built with parking in a convenient site near the town centre.

The senior partner, who had recently retired from my house, and moved to a village before his impending retirement, nearly had apoplexy. He shouted, "How dare you suggest knocking down the house where I started the Yeovil end!"

My predictions were not appreciated, and I was told that I had to carry on expanding Yeovil. They thought that my pay was ample enough, and If I was not happy with that?

I departed the room in disbelief that the partners did not realise that soon the Yeovil small animal end would become a massive part of the whole set-up in a few years and felt annoyed that my efforts for eighteen months were ignored entirely.

As Marie and I sat that evening wholly shocked by the outcome, she suggested I give my notice and set up my practice on the other end of town. I replied that the R.C.V.S. would never allow that, and it would be considered a very underhand move.

After a few days of annoyance at the ridiculous attitude to the expansion I had achieved at Yeovil, I started to think of contacting the R.C.V.S. It was unthinkable to work as a veterinary assistant in practice, leave the post, and set up opposition. I telephoned the secretary of the R.C.V.S. who told me that there would be a clause in my contract forbidding such a situation.

The paper side of the Sherborne Practice was not their strong point, and when I told the R.C.V.S. that I had never even seen a contract to sign, they were amazed. They said that there was nothing to legally stop me, although they strongly disapproved of the idea. I asked for this in writing, and my solicitor confirmed the state of affairs.

Incredibly, when Marie and I looked for large properties with space for a building and car park in a large garden, the very one leapt out off the page at us, on the main road on the other side of town.

The property was a large semi-detached Victorian house in two flats on the main A30 road into Yeovil from Sherborne. It was on a corner of a side road leading towards local beauty spot Wyndham Hill, which was eventually a dead end.

The property measured 90 yards to the end of the garden near Wyndham Hill. It concluded with an entrance into a garage. There was plenty of room at the end of the garden for Surgery Premises with a large car park, the entrance being from the side road.

Marie had an uncle and aunt who had just retired in Kilmarnock, and since they had no children, they were thinking of moving down to Yeovil to be near Marie and our children. They were very interested in moving into the downstairs flat since the upstairs apartment still had three bedrooms, enough for us. Since we would need a mortgage for the house, they offered to lend us money to build the veterinary premises and car park.

The house had been for sale for some time, and we acquired a mortgage. The sale went through quite quickly, and planning permission for the timber premises and the car park was given

Within two months, the building and the car park had almost been completed, and my present employers, who did not appear to have noticed the planning application received my months' notice. Since I still had over three weeks holiday due, it meant I only had to work for just over a week.

My employers did not seem too worried about my departure. Still, when I informed Robert Brown that I intended to start a practice on the other side of town, he was furious. He and the other partners tried their best to make my life miserable and threaten me with R.C.V.S. retribution. I pointed out that I had never had a contract and that I already had written confirmation from the R.C.V.S. that they could not legally stop me. I said nothing to any clients, and of course, the R.C.V.S. prohibited any advertising in those days.

We moved into the house, and I spent a frantic month buying veterinary equipment and decorating the new timber practice building. I wrote to every drug company, telling them of the new practice and asking for some drug samples.

They wanted my business, and I was swamped with visits from drug reps, thankfully giving me so many free samples that I soon had enough to open my doors.

At that time, Yeovil had a new hospital, and a client who was a theatre nurse rang and told me the old operating theatre was being demolished and arranged to meet me there.

I was amazed to see surgical instruments and other equipment, including dental ones, which were about to be thrown in a skip. I, therefore, exited with enough equipment in good enough condition to start my new venture!

My plate went on the property wall at the main road, and the following Monday, I opened my premises at 9 a.m. Gratefully, I found clients in the car park on day one. Many friends asked for dogs' toenails to be clipped and some vaccinations. The very kind gesture was much appreciated.

Somehow the bush telegraph worked well, and over the following months, a massive proportion of the clients from my previous position arrived to sign on as clients without me having spoken to any of them. So, May 1972 was an epic date in my life.

My position as an assistant vet was immediately advertised and very soon after quickly filled. The incumbent vet must have had a quiet time, as sooner or later, virtually all of the new clients I had obtained for the Sherborne practice over the years appeared at my new premises. Within a few years, my former employers sold the large house I had lived in to become an older people's home, and sheltered homes were built in my donkey's field.

They then built a purpose-built new veterinary practice building at that end of town. This event was pretty similar to my suggested plan, which they had earlier ridiculed. As a result, by 2020, there were five small animal practices in Yeovil.

Within a matter of months, it became apparent that most of the clients from the old practice had re-registered with me, without me speaking to them.

It was a pleasure to concentrate on pets only, though I missed the pleasant side of farm practice, especially delivering lambs and calves. To begin with, my Uncle Allan helped me as an assistant, and as a dog lover, he was very kind and polite. This kindness went down well with the clients, and Marie returned to teaching as Charlotte grew older.

Within a couple of years, I had paid back their loan, and our uncle and aunt moved to a nearby village.   Marie and I converted our house from two flats into one building and extended the lounge.

Chapter Thirty
My Practice

Apart from my table tennis playing cat, I soon encountered another amazing long-haired grey cat named George. By chance, I was at the reception when a car arrived. As well as the owners, a large grey cat walked with them from the car to the waiting room. To everyone's astonishment, the cat sat calmly beside them. Two clients grabbed their dogs, fearing an attack, on the other side of the waiting room.

When his turn came, George walked calmly into the consulting room with his owners. They lifted him on the table and suggested I should raise him into my arms. I did this, and he put his arms around my neck and hung on!

"Now that he has cuddled you, perhaps you would check his ears, as he has been shaking his head," asked the owner. In those days, ear mites were common in cats, and sure enough, my auroscope enabled me to see a few crawling in his ears.

The owners were horrified, but I showed them how to instil drops. I assured them that as long as they were put in weekly, the problem would be solved. So they told me they had a caravan at Charmouth and went there for holidays in the summer, taking George with them. Each day they would bring their chairs and blankets to the beach, where George would sit all day peacefully.

In those days, dogs were allowed on beaches, and frequently one would rush up in attack mode. George would sit passively till they were in range, then deliver a right hook into the face of the attacker, who usually ran off yelping in shock!

I never met another like him in all my career, and he was famous in his neighbourhood and at Charmouth, where the local dogs quickly learned to stay away from him.

Not long after this came probably the most distressing day of my career, I had a call from Yeovil police asking me to attend the main London railway line near a local village. As I climbed the embankment described on the phone, I could see a policeman beside the track.

He was distraught, and beside him lay a farm Border Collie wagging his tail. I was horrified to see that the London train had hit him and removed all four of his feet. But, amazingly, he had not bled to death yet and was in severe shock.

The officer held up a vein for me as I gave the euthanasia injection, and throughout, the poor soul's tail did not stop wagging, resulting in both of us in tears.

I returned the body to the nearest farm, and sure enough, they identified the collie as their excellent sheepdog. However, they were visibly upset and did think that a bitch at a neighbouring farm on the other side of the railway track could be in season. I will never forget that awful day as long as I live.

On the subject of animal parasites, I recall a visit to a Pekingese owned by an elderly couple living in a sheltered bungalow with a tidy garden. The wife was in a wheelchair where the little dog Peggy sat most of the day on her lap.

The poor dog showed typical symptoms of sarcoptic mange, common in those days, and often caught from urban foxes coming into gardens. As the owners were too old to bathe the patient, I suggested taking Peggy back to the surgery for appropriate baths formulated to kill the mites.

As I lifted Peggy from her lap, I noticed extensive lesions on her owner's wrists. I asked her how long she had had the problem, and she replied that the Dr. had been treating her eczema with ointment.

When I reached the surgery, I instructed the appropriate bath for the nurses to administer and managed to speak to the client's doctor. I explained that the dog had mange and lay on the lady's lap, near her exposed wrists most of the day. Peggy recovered after treatment, and I suggested that the couple stop feeding the "poor fox" they had seen in the garden. The Dr. appreciated my discreet phone call to him, and I noticed that the owner's eczema improved on further visits.

Around this time, my retired, widowed father had moved down to Yeovil and was happy to come in each day and help with bookwork and banking. My wonderful dad generously gifted me enough money to at last build substantial proper premises, with much more room and better equipment.

The new building and practice were renamed the Wyndham Hill Veterinary Centre, and I was very proud, as the new building attracted even more clients.

Since the sudden death of my mother, my father had by now spent several years alone. I did worry about him, especially when he retired young from his occupation as Head of Administration at Ayr County Council, which was to become part of a new Strathclyde area. He accepted a lump sum for early retirement since the area reorganisation wanted younger people in the fresh set-up.

During a long holiday with us, he met a widowed lady and remarried, living on the other side of Yeovil. Although he played a bit of golf and umpired at my cricket club, he suggested that he would like to come over to me each morning to do some bookkeeping and visit the bank each day. He enjoyed doing it, and I knew my books would be kept in a pristine office fashion.

A few years later, a situation occurred with similarities to the Pekingese case. Again, an elderly lady who lived in a flat with three cats that never went out had called in for flea treatment, including a spray of Nuvan Stay Kill to treat carpets. A few days later, the lady called in for three more cans of Nuvan Staykill, an Organo Phosphate compound that was banned a few years later as too dangerous.

The receptionist was sensible enough to call me to speak to the lady, and I explained that it was unsafe in a confined space to overuse the product, and if the cats never went outside, it was not likely they could have a flea problem.

She then showed me her arm, which had some fresh wounds on it. The lady then told me that the flea worms were in her bed and had been burrowing into her arms. She had been cutting them out with a razor blade, hence the wounds. I repeated my warnings to her and started a general conversation, in which I casually mentioned that her doctor would give her the same advice. I joked about not all doctors knowing much about cat fleas and casually asked which practice she used.

After she had gone, I notified all the staff that I was to be informed if the client returned for more sprays. I then telephoned the medical practice, and after a short time, her doctor telephoned me. I told him the story, explaining the lady was now self-harming but deluded about the flea worms. He told me he would visit her that day and resolve the situation, thanking me for bringing it to his attention. After that, I did see her cats again, and she never again asked for any flea treatment.

At the same block of flats, on another occasion, I did a house call to an elderly gentleman who owned a West Highland Terrier with eczema. The district nurse was visiting him as I arrived, and I had known her since she and her husband used my local pub. As she was there first, I asked if she minded me waiting in the room. She replied that I would be interested in having a look at her patient's leg.

The elderly gentleman was very proud to have me as a witness to his treatment. My friend removed his dressing to reveal a sinus in the middle of his shin, which she cleaned up as it was discharging slightly, applied some powder, and put on a fresh dressing.

I then learned that a German bullet had caused it at the Somme battle in1916, and in the busy casualty station, he had refused an amputation. The overworked and stressed army surgeon told him it was his lookout, as he was too tired to argue with him, and he would die of gangrene. Amazingly, despite the mud and the uniform pieces, no doubt deep in the wound, he did not develop gangrene. He recovered, but the sinus persisted for decades and had been dressed weekly till that day. It had not stopped the brave man from leading an everyday working life, though the leg still gave him some discomfort with which he happily lived.

His little dog did not need a lot of treatment, but I gave it an injection and some tablets and told him that after seeing his leg and hearing his history, I was happy to provide it free of charge.

I had another client years later, an elderly gentleman who had a cat that seemed to become often injured in fights with its mates. One day he mentioned something about the last war, and when I questioned him about it, I found that he had been a prisoner of the Japanese, working on the Burma railway. He had suffered so much, returning home weighing six stones.

After treating his cat, I told the nurse that he was not to be charged anymore. He immediately returned to the consulting room to protest. I told him that one of my hobbies was reading military history, and I knew a lot about Japanese prisoners' treatment. So from now on, there would be no charge for any problems his cat had. My gesture was a measure of my regard for him and what he had suffered so that my generation could have a free life.

He did come back under these terms, and for years I would find produce from his vegetable garden appear outside the back door of my house. Bless him!

That summer in hot weather, we seemed to have a problem with wasps in a back storeroom. I decided to investigate and noticed something strange about a large vent in the wall. I found the entire wall space filled with a giant wasp's nest on pulling back the guard. Placing goggles over my eyes, I approached with a can of Nuvan Staykill, held my breath, and sprayed the nest thoroughly till I had to take a breath, and exit closing the door.

That afternoon I found the floor littered with dead wasps, and the entire nest had collapsed, and there was not a live wasp to be seen. Eventually, the Organo Phosphates were banned, and many farmers suffered after-effects from using similar compounds in sheep dip.

Chapter Thirty-One
Sad Times.

Marie had taught at a local secondary school for some years, then became the personal secretary at a local sheepskin firm for the late Paddy Ashdown, who became M.P. for Yeovil and leader of the Liberal Party, Baron Ashdown of Norton-sub Hamdon. Marie and I had carried on together for some years, though our marriage was in serious trouble. The children grew older, and the practice got busier, with more staff employed. However, Marie and I continued together till John was fourteen, Imogen eleven, and Charlotte eight when she finally announced that she was leaving me.

We had been married for fourteen years, and she was a good mother to our children. Still, I always felt that she had been frustrated being married to someone with a high-profile occupation in our early years. Since she was knowledgeable, she missed having a career of her own, whether as a professional actress or a solicitor, although she had taught part-time for years. When we were first engaged, she had been offered a position as an announcer with the B.B.C but instead chose to marry and come to Cornwall with me. I often thought she would have made a great barrister, as I never stood a chance in any arguments with her!

At Ayr Academy, her teachers told her that she had the highest mark attained that year in Scotland in her Higher English leaving certificate. However, she did teach and carry on with an amateur repertory company. After our divorce, she qualified as an accountant and became a company director.

We arranged joint custody, with the children staying with me all week and going to Marie Saturday morning, returning Sunday evening. The children had to tolerate my basic cooking, but they coped incredibly well with a difficult situation, with the girls helping, as we struggled on as well as we could. It was a massive shock to the children, and they amazingly accepted the situation with courage, especially the girls.

So now weeks were so different with the children around. The house was so empty on the weekend when I was suddenly on my own, apart from the animals for company.
Fortunately, I still had my social life weekends at my local pub.

Barely fifty yards away was the White Horse, and all weekend bands played there, and I loved listening to the music with a beer in my hand. I still played the guitar, and one evening asked the lead guitarist of my favourite band if he would give me some lessons.

The following week Dave came round to my house and asked me to play and sing a few songs. Each time I stopped, he asked me to carry on and finally announced that he considered I was an excellent singer and rhythm guitarist and that instead of lessons, he offered me a place in his band. He explained that the present rhythm player and singer wanted to leave.

By now, another solo vet had started a practice in Sherborne and had already contacted me to discuss sharing emergency calls at weekends. Since he was elderly, all he wanted was a day off in the week in exchange for doing emergency evening weekend calls, as he did not go out at these times.

For days, Dave came to my house each weekday evening, and we practised a new band routine of numbers, and the current singer allowed me to do a few songs each night before he finally left. Within a month, I was in the four-piece band, which I renamed Flying Circus.

Suddenly my life changed as I ran my practice, looked after the children during the week, and played music when the children were with my now ex-wife on weekends. We remained on friendly terms, which assisted the situation with the children. The Sherborne vet took my emergency weekend calls, and I took him for a whole day each week.

Our divorce had gone through, and I purchased a lovely house for Marie on the other side of Yeovil, where she now lived with her long-standing boyfriend, whom she eventually married.

It was a sad time for me and difficult for the children, but I still played cricket. However, I did pull out of Round Table, as divorce was not as acceptable then as it is now.

I still play golf with former Round Table friends, but I found new friends in the music scene around the White Horse, where weekends found many local musicians together.

One of my musical friends, Phil, told me he was leaving to live in Jersey to make the grade as a full-time musician. He felt bad about leaving his girlfriend behind and asked if I would give her the chance to come round on weekends to venues with my band since we usually had a few camp followers with us wherever the band played.

I already knew his attractive girlfriend Loraine, and she became part of the regular band crowd.

I thought little of it for two months, and one day asked her how Jersey was progressing for her friend. She answered that he was doing well, had no plans to return to Yeovil, and even joked that she expected he had several new girlfriends by now!

A few weeks later, a crowd of us went to a friend's house after we played in the White Horse. I was sitting beside her when suddenly her hand touched mine, and although I was shocked at the time, it was the start of forty-odd years together.

I learned that she had been married young, was divorced, and had a little son Shaun, and now lived nearby with her widowed mother. So I arranged to take her out for a meal at a lovely restaurant at a local private club. Unfortunately, I had a night call the previous day, followed by another hectic day, followed by chairing a committee meeting at the cricket club early evening, which seemed never-ending. We finally made it to the restaurant by ten o'clock, romantically dimly lit with candles on the table and pleasant background music.

After the main course, the waiter arrived with the sweet menu, and Loraine made her choice. He then asked me to choose but got no response. I was so tired, and I had fallen asleep! Despite this inauspicious start, our friendship blossomed, and knowing my situation, Loraine offered to come round to my house after she had finished work to cook a meal for us all.

This soon became every evening in the week, and the children were delighted to have excellent meals once more, and weekends they went to stay with Marie. After a few months, the children started hinting that Loraine should move in, which soon happened, and eventually, her son Shaun joined us.

My children were very kind to Shaun, and with new friends, he was soon happy in his new home. Since the arrival of Loraine, the house was spotless, school uniforms pristine for Monday mornings, and a happy household soon returned. As time went on, I realised how lucky I had been to meet Loraine and realised that finally, I had met my perfect soul mate with which to share a happy life.

When we were first together, I was thirty-seven, and Loraine twenty-three. Many eyebrows were raised in Yeovil, but soon all the doubters were proved wrong. We married three years later, and the children accepted it happily. I came to regard Shaun as one of the family, and he grew up with his mother's kindly nature into a fine young man.

Loraine started helping me with emergency evening operations and showed the same affinity with animals as she did with children, with her calm, kind nature reassuring my patients. Her kindly way with frightened patients and common sense during emergency surgery was a great help to me. In time she took over as my leading surgical assistant, working each morning, and she quickly learned everything required of her. As a result, I always felt more confident operating with her than with the qualified nurses we had as time went on.

We adored all our pets, and the dogs all had good temperaments. But, sadly, we had no luck with our Bearded Collies, which we loved, and our last one, Bonnie, was difficult to breed. After several mating attempts, she finally gave birth to only two pups. Both of the puppies were already promised to friends, and by the time they were six weeks old, her health mysteriously deteriorated.

She was only three years old, and in desperation, I referred her to Bristol University Vet School, where an inoperable brain tumour was diagnosed, a condition incredibly rare in canines. I brought her home, and within days, euthanised her on my study carpet in Loraine's arms, and as the final injection entered her vein, all we could hear was the thump of her tail wagging and banging on the carpet. It is one of our worst moments and a particularly loved pet.

I should not say that, as all nineteen dogs were remarkable, and Loraine and I still talk of all of them to this day, as the bond between dog and owner can be such a strong one. They give such devoted love always.

We had two German Shepherds, both with excellent temperaments, and bred Tanya.
Incredibly, she reared thirty-three puppies in three litters and did not lose a single one.

When she was due for the first litter, I was at Edgbaston with my father, watching a test match against Australia. Loraine expertly delivered thirteen puppies, with the help of her friend Teresa whose main job I later found was being in charge of the bottle of wine in our heated whelping shed.

As the last pup was celebrated, Teresa decided to call the cricket ground, and Loraine was unaware this had happened. She told the secretary that I was a vet, and she had a most urgent message for me. The County Secretary had warned that only genuine emergencies warranted an announcement. Somehow, she managed to convince the gentleman to make an announcement at the end of an over for me to attend the secretary's office urgently. I knew that my son was driving back to the university that day, and it was a long walk around the ground to the office, and I feared the worst.

Thankfully, the secretary withdrew to the other side of the room when I returned the phone call. Teresa informed me that Tanya had delivered thirteen puppies. I immediately told her that I would deal with the emergency and told Teresa not to call back. I thanked the secretary, apologising profusely, and left him wondering what dreadful event I was about to attend. Dad and I made our way back around the ground, and poor Teresa had a rocket from me on our return.

Amazingly, at Tanya's third and last litter, she suffered uterine inertia, and though hormone injections brought more pups, in the end, the last three were delivered by caesarean section. So the only time I ever performed a caesarean on a German Shepherd dog had to be my own.

Years later, Tanya collapsed on her way home from a walk one day. Though she quickly regained consciousness, I noticed her eyelid mucous membranes were white, indicating an internal haemorrhage. On examining her, I palpated an apparent liver cancer.

That weekend, since she was failing but still eating, Loraine and I took her on her own for a weekend at a country hotel in Devon. Unfortunately, we did not know that the hotel had a resident peacock. As we walked to the front door through a garden, he emerged behind a bush and immediately displayed his plumage a couple of yards from Tanya.

She reacted in terror for the first time in her life but enjoyed the rest of her slow walks, and within a week, her decline was pronounced. However, I did not want her to die with another haemorrhage when we were perhaps out of the house, so that day, I euthanised her in Loraine's arms, happily eating a piece of raw sirloin steak.

Chapter Thirty-Two
Hypocrite?

Opposite the entrance to our car park on the other side of the road was a huge Victorian house, where an elderly gentleman lived alone. Every day he would go for a short walk with his black Labrador bitch, and sometimes talked to me.

He had run a clothing business and was notorious for not liking to part from his money except every evening when he would walk to the Royal Marine, another pub nearby. He commented on my busy car park more than once, being disgusted at my clients wasting their cash on family pets.

One day, he appeared in the waiting room telling me his bitch was eight years old and off her food. After a season, she had a huge abdomen and all the typical symptoms of Pyo metritis, which was a severe problem.

I explained that unless she had a hysterectomy, she would die within a week. I was then taken aback when the gentleman begged me to operate that day, telling me that he was not concerned about how much it would cost!

The Labrador made a good recovery and lived for several more years. When the owner finally went into a home, the beautiful old house was sold and became Beaumont House flats and a car park.

I knew it was built in the nineteenth century for the head surgeon at Yeovil Hospital and had stables behind it for his pony and trap, and his servant would drive him every day to work. The house was huge, with live-in servants and a tennis court in the vast front garden. As it was being demolished, I looked into a marvellous oak panelled dining room, and standing there, wondered what conversations must have taken place with colleagues at dinner parties at the end of the nineteenth century.

No doubt, Lister's discoveries of antisepsis must have come up with the advice to wash hands before rather than after the operation. Similarly, what did the surgeon think of using chloroform before amputating legs etc.? I stood in the room, trying to imagine the discussions that must have taken place.

Finally, the roof tiles of the replacement flats were placed by three young lads, and that particular morning Loraine and I were castrating a large adult dog.

At the critical point of the operation, they were sitting having their lunch on the roof, with a grandstand view of the proceedings opposite, showing great interest. Loraine assisting me, finally held up two large canine testicles to the window, dangling from artery forceps. All three stood up grimacing and holding their groin area, dangerously dancing around the rooftop.

Despite warnings about the demolition, the children had a good look after the workmen had departed in the evening. This resulted in Imogen appearing with a piece of planking attached to her foot by a nail, which I removed, cleaned up, and Loraine took her to A & E for a tetanus injection.

I had been told that when thousands of Americans occupied Yeovil before D Day, the old house was the home to U.S army pilots. One night they went on an alcoholic bender in Yeovil and carried on drinking in the lounge on return.

One, who had had enough, went upstairs to bed, which did not please his mates, resulting in one producing his revolver and firing through the ceiling! As the lounge was being dismantled, I checked the rafters and could see two bullet holes at one point.

One task that never got easier was euthanising animals, whether large or small.

When I first came to Yeovil, my boss Robert Brown asked me to assist in euthanising an elderly pony belonging to the daughter of a wealthy client at a large house in town. We arrived to find that a mechanical digger had dug an enormous hole in the garden near the house. Fortunately, the daughter was at school, and I helped position the pony beside the grave. My boss then shot the pony with the humane killer as I assisted the father by pushing the collapsing animal into the hole.

I had always refused to use such an implement of death, and this event was fifty-one years ago. I wonder if the present owners of the house realise that a pony is buried in the garden just outside their dining room window.

Years later, I recall visiting a lady near Yeovil with an elderly Border Terrier at the end of his days, and we agreed to euthanasia. Usually, I took Loraine to assist with the intravenous injection needed on such visits, but on this occasion, the client had asked that I go alone.

She held the friendly little dog while I clipped his front leg to make it easier to make the intravenous injection. Without advice, the lady held the leg correctly positioned before the final injection. Then, as I poised with the loaded syringe in my hand, she said, "My late husband was a vet. If you miss this vein, I'll bloody kill you!" This dire warning increased my pressure by 100% as the needle successfully entered the vein, and the little fellow went off to sleep peacefully.

Another client who insisted on holding up the vein for euthanasia of his old Scottie was a vicar, and I described what was required, which he dutifully managed well. I usually asked the owner, if they wished, to quietly reassure the patient, and instead of this, the vicar launched into a loud prayer. Unfortunately, he was concentrating so much on this that he had relaxed his grip on the patient. As the lethal dose of barbiturate took immediate effect, the Scottie's head collapsed, hitting the table with a small bang, interrupting his prayer.

"What's happened?" he cried.

"Well, the old fellow has gone off peacefully," I replied.

"He can't be dead already?" cried the Vicar and started vigorously shaking the deceased patient. Assuming that in his career, he had probably been present at several human deaths, I was astonished by his bizarre reaction, and he took some convincing that his pet had passed away.

With Loraine assisting me, I visited an elderly Labrador in a final collapse on a lounge floor on another occasion. The owner explained her husband was an airline pilot, flying at that moment, and two children sat on the carpet near the patient. They were a little girl aged about six and a little boy about four years old.

As I was just about to give the final injection with Loraine's help, I hesitated as the mother started to talk to the children explaining exactly why this was happening and how the dog would be at peace and go to heaven. I let her finish her gentle talk before giving the final injection. The children silently stroked the dog for a moment at their mother's suggestion. Finally, the four-year-old boy looked up and announced, "Good! Does that mean that *now* I can finally have a rabbit?"

My best vet student friend Dai lives in Chandlers Ford, and his three small boys had a guinea pig who died. The little lads were upset, so burial was made in the garden, and they were assured where the guinea pig would go after death. A week later, at breakfast, the oldest boy asked how long it would take for the guinea pig to go to heaven since they had just investigated his grave, and he was still there?

Another extraordinary tale is regarding an old German Shepherd that had survived a major operation to remove a back tumour, and although it was malignant, had survived another year. The owner, a widow, was devoted to the dog, and I had quite a difficult task to get her to agree to euthanasia, though metastasis now made this necessary.

Often the owner argues that the dog is not in pain as he did not cry out, and my argument back was usually around the fact that an animal would sometimes cry if you pulled a hair, but a patient severely lame with a broken leg did not, though in great pain.
Euthanasia was carried out, and at the owner's request, I carried the body and placed it on a blanket in the large hatchback outside, assuming home burial. However, as I passed her on my way back in, she was paying her account, and she turned and told me she wished to have the dog cremated. She then asked when we closed and told me she wanted to drive the dog down to the scene of his favourite walk near the coast!

I was astonished, and by the time she arrived later that hot afternoon it was not a pleasant task to lift the dead patient from the car to the large freezer to await the weekly Pet Crematorium visit.

Loraine and I sometimes go to the Marquis of Lorne, a hotel near Bridport owned by Bobby and Phillipa, and enjoy their fine food.

137

Over the years, we got to know them, and eventually, they acquired one of our German Shepherd dog's puppies. That Saturday, we were due to go there. I was in the consulting room with a rather posh client from Sherborne, examining her cat at that morning surgery.

Suddenly, my receptionist popped her head around the door, apologised for interrupting me, saying, "The Marquis of Lorne is on the phone". I picked up the receiver beside me, saying, "Yes, Bobby, we will be along for supper around 8 p.m. We look forward to seeing you." My client's jaw dropped, and for a moment, she lost track of the conversation.

Around this time, a large kennel six miles away was taken over by a Londoner who obtained permission to turn it into quarantine kennels. As I already was his vet, he offered me the business of taking over the work for the Ministry of Agriculture.

In previous practices, I had done a lot of T.B. testing for the Ministry, so they accepted me for the work, which entailed attending once a day for six days a week to inspect the health of the inmates.

When a dog arrived, it needed an examination and two rabies vaccinations a fortnight apart, then was released six months later. Owners were allowed to visit, and some did, which seemed to do nothing more than upset both parties.

Each day, the required visit made me consider that I had enough turnover to take on an assistant vet, and the work was primarily uneventful. I had a small consulting room to work in and give any treatment, including surgery, and I did several serious operations there. Apart from that, life was reasonably routine apart from two incidents.

One day a dog arrived from Canada via Heathrow, and I was amazed it was allowed into the country. I was informed that it was a cross between a German Shepherd and a Canadian wolf.

When the dog arrived, Simon, the kennel owner, told me that they had got it out of its crate straight into its pen, but every time they tried to open the door, the dog flew at the staff in a rage, and his kennel girls were terrified. So finally, since dart guns were in their infancy, we decided to open the kennel, holding an old door between us, and managed to crush the dog against a wall.

Any examination was impossible, and I managed to lean over as a kennel maid handed me the rabies vaccine syringe. I gave this, and we retreated behind the old door out of the kennel as quickly as was possible. From then on, food was swiftly pushed under the door with water. Since reliable canine sedatives were not available those days, I phoned the Ministry asking for advice about a safer way to give the second vaccine in two weeks. I was asked to phone back when another Ministry vet was available, and over the next few days, I spoke to several at Taunton. Each referred me to another and appeared strangely not to be interested.

Finally, I was so exasperated that I told the most senior vet that they would have to come and do it themselves if they wanted the second vaccine dose given. But, mysteriously, I heard no more from them, and the second dose was never given. To everyone's relief, the dog kept healthy for six months and was released into a cage which the owner from London put in his Land Rover and drove off.

This incident prompted me to order a dart blowpipe that zoos used to fire a syringe and needle containing a new drug named Immobilon, capable of dropping a dog. At last, the blowpipe arrived after a relatively long wait. Finally, the syringe could be fired attached to the dart, which had wool at the tail end.

I connected it carefully in my kitchen with a syringe and no needle and was very suspicious that it was powerful enough to work. But then, Loraine bent down to get something under the sink on the other side of the long room, and I had a perfect target!
I aimed, blew hard, and was amazed as the dart flew at speed, registering a loud, direct hit! Unfortunately, Loraine did not know there was no needle attached and eventually saw the funny side of my prank.

As instructed, a carpenter built a secure cupboard with a hefty padlock, and I wrote to the Chief of Yeovil Police to register the blowpipe. By return, I had a letter telling me he would not tolerate having such an apparatus in his patch, and it must be destroyed immediately. Knowing that I was allowed to have a blowpipe as a veterinary surgeon registered with the Ministry of Agriculture, I wrote to the then Home Secretary. I was triumphant to have a return copy of his letter to the Yeovil Police Chief saying it was legal, as long as the secure cupboard was inspected, which it soon was. Thankfully I never had to make use of it.

The second incident was the unexpected death of an elderly Labrador. I knew that this meant a post-mortem on the premises, with a Ministry vet as a witness. I also knew that the animal's head would need to be sent to the Ministry laboratory in Weybridge to be checked for the rabies virus. So, with my post-mortem equipment and a sterilised saw, I awaited the arrival of the Ministry vet.

He was horrified that I had already carried the poor old Labrador onto my consulting room table and returned to his car, re-emerging sometime later dressed in what looked like equipment similar to Neil Armstrong on the moon. He considered my dress of a plastic apron and surgical gloves inadequate and told me I examined at my own risk! He insisted on watching the autopsy through the consulting room window while he stood outside. The poor old dog had cancerous lesions in his kidneys. He was a dear old fellow that I had seen every day for the last five months, and although ageing fast, had shown no symptoms of his sickness. I had the unpleasant task of removing his head and placing it in the Ministry vet box.

I always felt that bringing elderly animals from abroad under stress, then virtually imprisoning them in solitary confinement for six months was cruel. After a few years, the kennels were sold to a new owner, a retired lady from London, also a dog breeder. She and her lady companion owned, bred, and showed so many German Shepherds and Shid Tzus that they transported them from London to Yeovil in a hired double-decker bus. Her companion was a very knowledgeable lady. Every time I had to treat any of their animals, she continually tried to tell me what to do, appearing to consider that she knew more than I did.

For a few months, I tolerated the situation. Then, one day the two ladies arrived at my premises with one of their stud dogs, a large, long-haired male German Shepherd who had fought with another dog and suffered a horrendous bite causing a massive tear in the skin of the elbow several inches long.

I told them it needed to be shaved, cleaned properly, then sutured, possibly with a drainage aperture. The ladies immediately said to me that the dog had been imported from the U.S.A. and had cost a lot of money. They, therefore, did not want to risk a general anaesthetic and wanted the repair done under local anaesthesia. They were breeding from it because of his excellent conformation, and I told them I thought the size of the wound made this an impossibility. Since the animal was young and fit, I would be happy to anaesthetise him every day for a week if necessary. I was surprised that the owner could not agree, and they insisted on their plan. I stood my ground and told them if they did not want a general anaesthetic, they should find another vet. They stormed out, and I was pleased to resign the quarantine kennel contract to a neighbouring practice, who were happy to accept the blowpipe.

Around this time, Shaun, who was about twelve, won a goldfish at a fairground at Sherborne, where the family enjoyed an evening. Although I felt a solitary goldfish in a bowl a cruel life, I relented, and he studiously took over its welfare, feeding and cleaning its water.

After a year, his enthusiasm diminished, and Loraine ensured that the poor fish was fed. Then, one morning after the children had gone to school, Loraine found the goldfish dead, so she buried him in the garden and left the bowl in place, telling the other children, but not Shaun. A month later, Shaun arrived at the breakfast table and shouted, "My goldfish has disappeared!" This statement brought a round of applause from the other children, who already knew the fate of the goldfish. Loraine informed him that it had died a month before. Every morning for weeks afterwards, he was greeted at the breakfast table with enquiries about the health of his goldfish.

We also had two cats, a black cat called Maggie, who was very solitary, and a real mouser, frequently leaving mouse tails around the house, and Imogen's favourite Brian, a white and tabby, who was the complete opposite and gave the impression that he would have run for his life if confronted by a rodent. He loved to sleep all day and pestered the girls to cuddle him, not appearing to have a great interest in life.

As a teenager at Yeovil College doing her A levels, Imogen painted a brilliant watercolour of Brian, which is still on the wall of our house.

One favourite occupation was delivery of new puppies, and one evening a German Shepherd bitch came in with uterine inertia, a hormonal disorder. She already had three live pups but refused to strain any more. Since it was night time, and I knew the bitch was friendly, I decided to admit her, and every half hour Loraine and I gave her a hormone injection resulting in more puppies.

I thought she might have more. We had a sizeable and clean whelping box in the house, so I walked the dog down my garden and into the house. We placed her in our large bathroom, and Loraine put the puppies in with her. Two more checks in the night, and two more injections, produced two more pups, and she seemed pretty content with six, allowed me to palpate her abdomen, and I was confident the births were over.

Leaving the light on, I left her happy, and we grabbed a couple of hours of sleep. At six a.m. I wandered through and called her by name. Before I got a yard into the room, she flew out of the box and sank her teeth in my hand.

I retreated, closed the door, and found a tear with a patch of skin hanging down on my right palm. Loraine was horrified and told me she would drive me to casualty.

"I have a better idea," I said, and we dressed and went up to the operating theatre, where Loraine cleaned the wound. My first boss told me to give injections with both hands and practice on any recumbent cattle many years ago. So, thanks to his advice, I used my left hand to inject a local anaesthetic into my wound, then I brought the flap back into place with five sutures, and Loraine also scrubbed as she tied the knots.

The happy owner collected the mum and puppies from my bathroom the following day with Loraine's help, and she was never told what had happened.

Two days later, I found myself getting fuel at the local garage, with our family doctor at the next pump. I told him what had happened, and I showed him my wound. He thought it was a neat job. "Some poor intern should be grateful!" he laughed.

Chapter Thirty-Three
Unusual Incidents

One New Year's Eve party in our local White Horse, everyone was very merry by midnight when the landlord found me and told me one of the barmen had cut his hand on a glass. He took me through to the kitchen where the sink was full of red water, and some helpful friend of the barman was swabbing the wound. Having kicked the friend out, I acquired a clean towel to hold on to the injury and told the landlord it must be sutured.

He replied that the ambulance service was impossibly busy at this time, and the barman was too drunk to walk to the hospital. Also, since it was New Year's Eve, none in the pub had a car, and taxis were impossible to acquire unless booked weeks before. He then enquired if I would treat it, and the barman said he thought the patient could manage to stagger to my nearby premises.

I then took him across the road to my nearby surgery and cleaned the wound. I printed out on a page of headed paper saying he permitted me to suture the damage at his own risk, and he happily signed it, making it legal. A little local anaesthetic, and ten minutes later, I had closed the wound with a few sutures. Unfortunately, the patient was so intoxicated, and I felt the drug was hardly needed. He slept the night soundly in an armchair in the pub, and a week later, I removed the sutures as the wound had healed perfectly.

On another New Year's Day, I had a friend with a painful loose incisor who could not get anyone at A.& E. to help, as no dentist was available, and they did not consider his situation an emergency. He appeared at lunchtime that day, and after a little local anaesthetic, I pulled it out for him, and he left happy.

Over the years, we had many lovely dogs, from Shetland Sheepdogs, Bearded Collies, and later bred German Shepherds and Yorkshire Terriers simultaneously, and you can add to that three Chihuahuas. Unfortunately, at least three of our dogs had arrived in the surgery after the death of an owner, and we were asked to rehome them, including a dear old, almost blind Sheltie, whose owner went into a home.

By the time the girls were teenagers, I had employed them part-time on Saturday mornings, and this incredibly resulted in two more Chihuahuas in quick succession. At one time, we had four children, seven dogs, two cats, an enormous black rabbit, and hamsters, which poor Loraine had to manage and help a husband with a veterinary practice. How did she manage?

The rabbit was a giant called Basil, and I spent much time repairing his hutch, from which he regularly escaped. Next door to us was a guest

house, and one day I awoke and found a note on my back door, saying, "There is an illegal immigrant in my greenhouse!"
I retrieved Basil from his latest escapade, breakfasting on lettuce and cucumbers in the greenhouse.

One of the girls' hamsters escaped from its cage, and after some weeks, we assumed that our black cat Maggie had been responsible. She was a hunter, unlike our dopey tabby and white Brian, who would probably have run away afraid of it.

A few weeks later, Loraine noticed that the children's pyjamas were chewed up in a drawer, and we suspected the hamster might be still around, and Maggie had not found it yet. Then, a few days later, an elderly carpet layer came to fit a new stair carpet and left the new roll lying in the house before removing the old one.

Eventually, he unrolled the new one and almost had heart failure when a hamster shot out under his nose and ran into the girls' room. However, it was soon captured and lived another year.

Imogen had another hamster which was found sitting on a bench at the local bus station. She named him Aspel and found he did not bite and was very happy to be handled, living to old age.

I acquired a new client who lived with his servant in a massive house near Crewkerne. He was retired and had a Labrador with chronic flea dermatitis. In the late thirties, the owner contracted osteomyelitis and underwent surgery to shorten his legs, removing diseased bone. On a cabinet in his lounge was a signed photograph of Sir Alexander Fleming since he was one of the first patients in the U.K. treated with Penicillin. He was an amazing man, and thrilled to learn that, like his idol Fleming, I was also an Ayrshire man.

Many other local practices had treated the Labrador, and at last, my diagnosis and treatment for flea allergy dermatitis cured the dog, and he was very grateful. If I was ever in the area on visits, I popped in for the sherry always on offer and found that his factory in London had produced most of the cotton wool used in the second world war in Britain.
He was a brilliant man, and I was astonished at what he had achieved after the appalling surgery he had endured before the discovery of Penicillin.

Chapter Thirty-Four
Holidays

We had some fantastic family holidays when I employed a locum, giving me a chance to escape from work pressures. We successfully holidayed together in Jersey, Ibitha, and particularly the Greek Islands.

One year the family holiday was in a nice hotel in sunny Majorca, where we spent many hours at the swimming pool, overlooking a rocky promontory. Charlotte, now aged four, was a particularly outgoing personality and quickly became friendly with two elderly ladies who sat every day on the opposite end of the pool. They were Austrian and spoke enough English to enjoy Charlotte's attention.

Unfortunately, John had discovered a nearby shop that sold imitation stick-on tattoos. So soon, all three were sporting a tattoo somewhere on their bodies, despite my efforts to discourage them.

The following day, Charlotte swam up to our end of the pool with one of her elderly friends, and as usual, we exchanged greetings. Then, as they stood together, holding onto the side of the pool, Charlotte suddenly grabbed her companion's wrist, held it up and shouted, "Look! my friend also has a tattoo!"

Stunned silence ensued as Loraine and I recognised a wartime concentration camp number on her wrist. As her friend burst into tears, Charlotte was shocked and swam back to the other end of the pool, resulting in Charlotte crying, not knowing why she had upset her. By now, the elderly ladies had disappeared, and we explained the situation to the children.

Later in the day, I encountered the Austrian ladies enjoying coffee in the hotel. I quietly explained the pretend tattoos and how we had explained the situation to the children and that Charlotte was distraught. Both of the ladies had been children in Auschwitz during the last war and were the only survivors of their families.

I quietly spoke of our horror, explained how sad I was to hear of the rest of their family, and talked about how my father had been wounded and disfigured in the war. To them, it meant that both families had suffered, though ours in a relatively minor way.

The following day, Charlotte walked around the pool to them and was soon enveloped in their arms as she sobbed again after being comforted for the rest of our stay. The three of them spent many hours together, and they told us she was a lovely child.

I would have loved them to know that Charlotte would go to London to the Blue Peter studios to accept a Child of Achievement award for voluntary work with disabled children in her teenage days. Then, later in her career win an annual prize for caring and inventive work as a sister in Yeovil Hospital.

One year Imogen had become interested in seeing Ayr in Scotland, where I was brought up. I pointed out that although it had a sand beach and was a lovely town, the weather could not compare to going abroad. She won the day, and we incredibly had the only heatwave in the many year's history of the town and a great time in a holiday chalet near Ayr.

When Loraine and I went on holiday alone, we often visited Greek Islands, and for years flew to Athens, then to the port to catch ferries to the islands. Every ferry was usually met by locals offering accommodation, so we would stay a few days, then grab a ferry to another island, ensuring that we ended up at Athens in time for the return journey. We had fabulous times, and over the years, we visited over thirty islands. We only had one bad moment, when returning to the airport our flight was not showing.

Since this was nearly forty years ago, few Greeks spoke English, and we eventually found the basement of the airport, filled with many Greeks at desks. But, again, none could understand us, which resulted in Loraine bursting into tears.

Being an attractive young woman, she was soon surrounded by people comforting her, and a young man announced in English that our Airline had failed in our absence! He was in charge of fuel supply at the airport and telephoned London, telling us that if we watched in 24 hours, a notice would be displayed for London tickets. This display eventually happened, and we were given tickets for the following day on a scheduled Kenya Airlines flight. We were very relieved as we boarded, and the aircraft was an old Boeing 707. Unfortunately, this occurred long after they were no longer in use, and most were sold to third-world countries.

Few of the overhead lockers had doors, some were hanging off, the carpets were worn out, the announcements were inaudible with a crackling system, and we took off - terrified! Fortunately, though, we landed safely after one of the strangest breakfasts I had seen. It consisted of what appeared to be a white omelette and large black beans. Loraine was horrified, and I ate both portions.

Again, about thirty years ago, we went on a Mediterranean cruise, when cruising was first brought to non-wealthy people by Airtours in the eighties. Our first dinner with five couples, and gentlemen in jackets and ties, produced a strange incident.

Sitting opposite me was an elderly gentleman wearing a Somerset County Cricket Club tie. He and his wife were from Bridgwater, and he was great fun. At one point, someone started asking around the table about occupations, and all the men replied. Those days, most ladies were housewives, and there was a surprise when one announced loudly that she worked as a counsellor.

Someone asked if she worked for her local council, and all at the table were mystified, so she gave a long talk about the work she did, including helping people after bad experiences. When she finished her lecture, the little fellow opposite us, Kenny, told her that her job sounded very interesting. She replied that if he needed help, to please talk to her after the meal.

To everyone's surprise, Kenny replied, "I will tell you a story. I once piloted a badly damaged Wellington back from the Ruhr, with my co-pilot dead beside me, my navigator bleeding to death behind me, after being hit by flack. I made it back to England and crash-landed miles from anywhere. I sat there for hours in darkness, by which time my navigator had died. I was unable to move with a broken jaw and two broken legs, till rescued at daybreak, and I didn't get bloody counselling!"

There was a stunned silence, with many trying hard to suppress laughter, while the lady and husband got up from the table and sat elsewhere for the rest of the trip. We enjoyed his hilarious company for the rest of the cruise with his lovely wife.

It seemed no time till the children were growing up, and we had to deal with teenage daughters wanting to go to discos underage "As all our friends are going!" but Loraine coped well with keeping an eye on them since a doting dad was not much help.

The boys were less trouble, though John had a birthday celebration near the end of his pre-university days and was in town one Saturday night in December. So we were in bed when at 2 a.m., the back doorbell rang, and Loraine answered with the dogs barking furiously.

She opened the back door into the conservatory. Two police officers walked in with a naked John kept respectable by a strategically placed police helmet. After a drunken night out, his friends had overpowered him and removed all his clothes, leaving him to walk home in that state with eventual assistance from the local constabulary.

In the children's younger years, I had played cricket for Yeovil, and they were happy to spend the day at the local ground. They had plenty of teammates' children to play with. Sometimes, even when older, they would come to private clubs where I played music in my band. Eventually, both girls went to Yeovil District Hospital and chose nursing as a career, while John left for university to study geology and joined the Territorial Army.

Shaun finally joined the Regular Army, and we proudly watched his parade at Aldershot as he won all three cups for new entrants.

One weekend he came home on leave and went to a disco in town with his friends. We were now getting used to being alone in our house since John was at university in Plymouth, and Shaun now living in quarters at Aldershot. At the same time, even the girls had moved into a flat across the road to have their freedom in their nursing careers and social life. We returned from our Saturday evening out and went to bed, leaving a small kitchen top window open if the German Shepherds and Yorkies were too hot in the summer weather. Then, around 2 a.m., the

146

dogs started barking furiously, and I got out of bed, grabbed my old cricket bat kept beside the bed in case of burglars, and rushed downstairs, forgetting to put my spectacles on. The dogs were barking at a head wearing a baseball cap as a body was trying to squeeze through the kitchen window. I opened the back door into the conservatory, then the outer door and the Shepherds flew outside, in attack mode. Suddenly there was silence, and as I stood in the kitchen, the dogs reappeared, wagging their tails and got back into their beds.

I then saw the baseball cap in the conservatory and a voice saying, "Boss! Boss! It's me, Shaun! I've forgotten my key!"

Shaun was doing well in the Army and was very fit, having played as a sixteen-year-old for Yeovil Town Reserves as a striker. He was chosen to represent his regiment in an Army competition climbing up Ben Nevis in a complete kit. Unfortunately, on the way down, his boots slipped, and as he fell, he tore his knee ligaments. So he was invalided out of the Army with a pittance of a pension and a soccer career at an end. He now works in I.T. and lives in Colchester with his lovely wife Jemma and children Charlie and Edamay.

John became a Captain in the T.A. in the Royal Welsh Regiment and served in Croatia. When the regiment was disbanded a few years ago, he was among the Territorial Army officers invited to a goodbye tea party at Buckingham Palace. I am proud of the picture of John at the palace standing behind the Queen, which hangs on our lounge wall.

John acquired a B.Sc. in geology and worked in offshore exploration gas rigs, examining samples brought up while searching for oil and gas, before taking two different M.S.C. degrees, and now works as a geologist specialising in checking nuclear radiation. He lives in Didsbury with his lovely wife, Daljit, a consultant anaesthetist at Stockbridge General, with their beautiful daughter Sara. He also played Rugby till age 50 and has just retired from the T.A.

The practice now had a part-time assistant vet in Dr Mark Newton-Clarke and was getting busier all the time, despite several other practices opening in town.

Chapter Thirty-Five
Sherborne

Yeovil was an expanding town, and before long, we opened a branch practice in Sherborne where Mark was born, and the new branch soon had many new clients there, thanks to his hard work and expertise.

One day we had a frantic call from a client, and Loraine and I left on a house visit, unusually armed with some sterilised surgical kit. The lady had hired a power vacuum to clean all her carpets in the house.

She had a lively Maltese Terrier dog, and as we entered the house, we could hear the dog screaming. He had come up behind her, and since the machine was noisy, she was not aware he was in the room. But, unfortunately, his long hairy tail had been caught in the vacuum, and at least half of the tail was inside the machine.

On examining the vacuum from underneath, I could see no way to open it up, so with Loraine holding the dog in a blanket, I managed to inject Immobilon into his leg. This enabled me to give enough anaesthesia to clip the leg, and Loraine cleaned the area. At the same time, I donned surgical gloves, opened my kit, and amputated the tail, temporarily closing the wound. Within minutes the little fellow was on the anaesthetic machine in my operating theatre, and I did another sterile amputation nearer his pelvis.
The dog recovered, and the lady returned the hired vacuum with part of a tail still in the mechanism!

A young man rang our back doorbell one Saturday morning and explained he was Martin Smith, the son of the late Eric and Pam in Stourport. It was hardly surprising that I did not recognise him, as it was thirteen years since I had known him as a young boy when he had his appendix removed. He told us he was passing on his way home from three months at work and asked us to guess his occupation. Loraine immediately thought of the ridiculous answer possible.

"You are a lighthouse keeper," she said.

His face was a picture, and he replied that he had just finished a spell at the Eddystone Lighthouse. It was great to hear of his life and all the news about Stourport.

One day we had a whelping case at 2 a.m. involving a Yorkshire terrier owned by a pleasant lady who lived in a nearby village.

The cervix was open on examining the little patient, and I suspected a large pup was the problem. However, the client was an experienced breeder and was relieved when I suggested a caesarean delivery, so I admitted the little Yorkie.

Loraine never minded having her sleep disturbed for a caesarean, her favourite operation. Soon she was resuscitating four lively puppies, including the first significantly large male, and soon mum was back in a pen with her babies. I telephoned the grateful owner, who was no youngster, and asked if I would keep them in till morning.

As we started to leave the recovery area, the little mother began to cry out every time Loraine left the room. Very soon, she was installed in our Yorkie whelping box in our bedroom, with a heat lamp above her. Still, she kept crying and was only happy to settle down on a vet bed blanket beside Loraine in our large bed. Satisfied, at last, she fed her puppies and settled down for what was left of the night.

The next day the grateful owner collected the happy family and was not surprised at the mother's behaviour. As a well-known breeder, she subscribed to "Dog World." Shortly after this incident, she read a letter to the editor saying that all modern vets had no compassion or care for their patients. They were only interested in making money.

She sent a letter of reply saying her Yorkie had had a caesarean delivery during the night and that the vet and his wife had been concerned that the little dog needed human reassurance and that the mother and litter had ended up in bed with the vet and his wife.
The next edition had two letters saying virtually, "I wish I had a vet like that!"

We have always had a cat, and I am a cat lover, finding them very inscrutable creatures who seem to dominate often their owners doing only what the cat wants and when it wants it. I have treated a cat in the morning twice in my career, only to have it brought in that evening for the same problem by different owners. Each time they had an address a few doors away. The first time, the two sets of owners accepted the cat was eating in two places and lived with it.

The second time, an unholy row developed over ownership, and since this was before the days of microchipping, I never found out the result.

Thankfully, we rarely had any exotic pets presented in my days of practice, but one day I had a call from the owner of a python that had a skin condition on its head, and the owner wanted a swab taken for a lab test. He seemed very knowledgeable on the subject, and I agreed to see him.

When he arrived with a large sack, I was shocked when he told me he had put the snake in his freezer for a few hours to slow him down. Then, I was horrified as he took out an enormous python and held his head to show me the problem.

I picked up the laboratory swab and looked at a nasty sore on its head. As I approached from the front, the snake was not too sleepy and was able to threaten me with his fangs. So I changed approach and took the swab from behind his head. A bacterial infection was confirmed, and thankfully an antibiotic skin ointment meant it healed.

149

When I was on holiday, I must admit that I rarely revealed my occupation since it tended to start anyone I spoke to talking endlessly about their pet's problems. I was on holiday to get a change of scenery.

Every year we have a holiday with the children. I was so grateful to Loraine for taking on the stepchildren's responsibility, and by now, we had married, so I used to also take a holiday for just the two of us.

One year we went to the Greek island of Spetse, where we immediately befriended a couple from Middlesbrough, George and Linda. George was a detective in the Cleveland police, and I did tell them I was a vet.

At that time, Spetse had no cars on the island, and travel to other beaches was by small boats which travelled all around the coastline. In addition, several locals operated decorated pony and traps, which would take you around the island on the available tracks.

That evening, we went out to a taverna with George and Linda, and they told us that they had a pleasant trip around the island that afternoon in such a carriage, which was a great success.

What they did not tell me was that they had revealed my occupation to the driver.

The following day, I had a call from the Hotel reception to tell me that someone at reception wished to see me. On arriving there, I found the driver of the pony and trap, who led me outside where three ponies were lined up. He explained there were no vets on the island, and one pony was off its food. I examined the pony and immediately saw the problem, a massive abscess on its neck. By now, I had an audience, including the hotel manager, who knew the driver well.

I explained what was needed, and the manager took me into the hotel kitchen, where I selected a suitable sharp knife and some paper towels. I cleaned the skin with some antiseptic taken from the hotel and asked the owner to hold the pony tightly. I cleared the increasing audience to a safe distance. Before the pony realised anything, I made a sharp cross-cut into the abscess, which spectacularly ejected a considerable amount of yellow pus into the drive to the astonishment and disgust of the watching hotel guests. I cleaned the area up with more towels, was happy that the abscess would drain and heal uneventfully over a couple of weeks, instructing the owner to bathe it every day to keep the wound open as long as possible but to watch out for flystrike.

He then asked me to look at the other two ponies, which were youngsters he had purchased at a recent mainland sale. I checked their teeth and estimated that one youngster was around 10 years old, and the other may be as old as15.

The driver's euphoria over the abscess and treatment without charge was somewhat tarnished by the knowledge of the ages of the other two.

One of the audience was the tour representative. She had come in to see a client who was staying in the hotel for a week. I was astonished when she revealed that not only was there no vet on the island, but no doctor either, and the local pharmacist gave most treatment. Unfortunately, however, a girl of about twenty, her client staying in the hotel, had gashed her leg while swimming on the first day of her holiday. She was diving off a rock and managed to strike another in the water below.

The representative asked me if I would accompany her to the client's room and examine her. As the door opened, I detected a dreadful odour of infection and found the girl with a large, grossly infected gash on her shin. I asked to see the antibiotics that the pharmacist had supplied and could see immediately that (maybe due to language difficulties) the dosage was that for a child. I told the representative that the situation was an emergency since the leg was well on the way to becoming gangrenous. Therefore, the girl must be taken immediately to a mainland hospital. The representative was most relieved, and that afternoon a helicopter landed and took her to hospital in Athens. Thus, within two days of arrival, I had already acted as island vet and island doctor.

I recall another holiday where I was delighted my occupation was revealed. We were on a night flight to Tenerife with another couple of good friends, and it was back in the days when cockpit visits were allowed. I had been in many cockpits since 1963, flown in small aircraft, and taken the controls of a two-seater.

Later in the flight, the two wives disappeared to the cockpit, being away for some time. I think the two pilots were probably enjoying the company of two attractive young ladies, slightly inebriated by that stage of the journey.

Eventually, they returned, and Loraine told me the captain wanted to speak to me about his dog. "You're joking! We are starting to lose height," I replied. "No! No!" She insisted, "It is serious, and you must go!"

Reluctantly I went to the front of the aircraft, and the cabin crew were relieved to see me and took me to the cockpit. The pilot told me that his wife rang to say she had just been to the vet with their 10-year-old Labrador bitch, who was very ill just before take-off. The vet diagnosed Pyometra, a closed septic uterus infection, and only a hysterectomy would save her life. However, without her husband present, she was unsure how to proceed and did not know if the dog was too old to survive a major operation.

I was able to tell him that surgery was the only option, the dog could live for several more years, and that she would be virtually back to normal in a couple of days. I strongly recommended that he immediately go ahead with the surgery. He was delighted, as his children were devoted to the dog, and on landing, he would ring his wife and ask her to go ahead with the operation.

He laughed and told me that he had always wanted to be a vet when he was younger.

I replied that I had always wanted to be an airline pilot. "Have you ever been in a cockpit before?" he asked.

I replied that I had been in many cockpits without really thinking, but I had never sat in on a landing.

The pilot looked at his co-pilot and told me that was forbidden. Then, following a pause, he continued, "But after the wonderful advice you have given me regarding my Labrador, you can strap yourself into the spare seat." I beamed as I obeyed, and over the next few minutes, he explained where all the controls were, and I was fascinated to see the radar showing the weather.

After this, he told me they were now on the final approach, and I must stay silent. So I sat back watching the tiny lights of Tenerife Island in the distance when suddenly the radar screen went blank.

"Damn! The radar has packed up!" exclaimed the pilot, and the co-pilot engaged in conversation with air traffic control. Meantime, I was aware that an airliner had crashed into Mount Teide a few years before with total fatalities.

Suddenly the pilot seemed to remember me and told me not to worry, as they knew where the mountain was, and if I looked ahead, I would soon see the runway. At first, I could only see the lights of towns, but soon saw the runway, which was getting closer at an alarming rate.

I was happily absorbed in the thrill of a lifetime and fine till the last second when the nose went up, and the power was killed. Suddenly the aircraft seemed to drop like a stone until the rear wheels made smooth contact. That last second of the drop took me by surprise, and I was not expecting it.

Nevertheless, I was so grateful to the pilot and stayed in my seat till the engines were switched off and all the checks were made. Loraine was unhappy about my failure to return to my seat and had to wait at passport control with my passport until I emerged with the crew, wearing a grin like a Cheshire cat after the thrill of a lifetime.

Chapter Thirty-Six
Foreign Bodies

I was once presented with a ten-year-old Dachshund with a four-inch diameter tumour
attached to the underside of his neck.   I was sure it was a substantial benign Lipoma, a harmless tumour of fat cells.

The owners lived many miles from Yeovil and had seen several vets, and none of them would operate on the little dog. But, incredibly, the little fellow got around by kicking the lump away from him with his foreleg and taking one step at a time.

I successfully removed the tumour, and it was heart-rending to watch him awake from the anaesthetic and suddenly start running around his recovery pen, a delighted little dog. His owners were overjoyed at his new lease of life.

Foreign bodies are a common problem and come in all shapes and forms. I recall a three-month-old kitten presented with a completely closed septic eye. I could see something in the eye trying to clean it up, but the pain was causing the kitten to struggle a lot. I anaesthetised the little patient, cleaned the eye out properly, and could see a tiny grey object.

Using an apparatus that had a highly lighted magnifying glass on a stand, I could immediately see the tip of a sewing needle. Then, using my tiniest forceps, I gently pulled a two-inch-long sewing needle from the eye that must have penetrated quite a distance into the brain! The owner told me that she had found the kitten playing in her sewing basket the day before, and later that day, she had first noticed him in distress.

Amazingly the eye healed well, and when I neutered him under anaesthetic a month later, his behaviour was quite normal, and no fluorescein stain was taken up by the cornea, showing the wound had healed.

Grass lawns in summer commonly become caught in the ear canals of dogs, particularly flop-eared breeds like Cocker Spaniels, and cause much distress. However, they are easily removed with crocodile forceps under general anaesthetic. Another common site is the upper aspect of the foot in dogs, with continuous licking, which causes significant distress for the patient. There is not a part or orifice that I have not removed a grass seed from, including the tongue, nose, anus, vagina, and penis.

One day I was confronted by a Black Labrador with a large marrow bone firmly lodged over his upper jaw, making him look comical. I could only assume that he had been attempting to remove the delicious marrow from within and somehow lodged it in a seemingly impossible situation. Unfortunately, none of the equipment I had was of any use in removing it, so I went down to the local Fire Station to ask for their assistance.

The friendly dog furiously wagged his tail when suddenly surrounded by a team of firemen, just eating delivered pizzas and due to go off duty. They had various ideas, and since I took Loraine with me, I got the dog on a table and anaesthetised him with intravenous Propofol, a quick-acting agent. (Amazingly, Propofol, the milky white solution now used worldwide to induce anaesthesia in humans, was discovered by Ian, later Professor Ian Glenn, whilst he worked for a short time at Imperial Chemical Industries.   Ian came from the Isle of Arran opposite my hometown of Ayr and was an intern at the Glasgow Vet Hospital, having qualified two years before I did.   His discovery earned him a world award in medicine, and he is an honorary fellow of the Royal College of Anaesthetists in the U.K.).

The firemen were very impressed and attacked the bone with ever more robust equipment until a massive cutter used on crashed cars cut through and released the bone. The whole episode took half an hour, and although they were now half an hour late for a skittle match in a nearby pub, none left till the dog was fixed.

They were then astonished when he awoke quickly and insisted on licking every firefighter enthusiastically, with his tail wagging non-stop, which made their evening. Then, finally, they departed, saying they had not enjoyed a "shout" so much in a long time!

Around this time, I reencountered the firemen while answering a police call one summer evening as it was starting to get dark.   Behind the main road in Yeovil was a set of garages.   A public member reported a group of people acting suspiciously near them, and a large fire had started.

The firemen found no one there when they attended and put out what appeared to be a deliberate fire near a garage. So they called the police, who then called a doctor.   Then the police called me, as some suspicious remains were found in the middle of the fire. When I arrived, the doctor showed me some burnt intestinal remains, and he wondered if it could be a baby. So I donned gloves, and together we examined the charred remains.

I soon found a charred foot, which I realised was a rabbit foot, gradually more singed rabbit hair, and eventually a charred rabbit head. The doctor was surprised how similar the burnt intestines were to human ones.   I made a statement to the police, who did not track down those responsible.   A rather spooky few moments, and I was glad to resolve the case satisfactorily.

Chapter Thirty-Seven
Strange Cases

I had a client whose hobbies included shooting and fishing. Amazingly, he did not like eating fish and would often bring large Trout as gifts when he appeared with his elderly Labrador.

Eventually, I euthanised his gundog and did not see him for several months. Then, one day he appeared, very excited, with a nine-month-old Labrador. He told me he had paid a lot of money for the dog, as it was already trained, and asked me to give him a thorough check-up.

He went shooting at a nearby village wood with his friends that weekend, expecting a good day out. Instead, on the firing of the first shot, his new dog bolted and was found three miles away later that afternoon in Sherborne main street, proving you don't always get a bargain.

Foreign bodies swallowed by dogs, and occasionally cats, always present a problem, and no two are ever the same. Usually, the patient is repeatedly vomiting and very unwell, and often the object can be palpated or shown on x-ray.

Delicate items like clothing are harder to detect and deal with, often meaning the bowel has to be opened in several places for things like string or chewed up clothing with which I often had to deal. Finally, the most common bones are always unsafe to give to animals, particularly chop or barbecue chicken bones.

However, I have removed children's toys, balls of all shapes and sizes, corn on the cob, a condom, socks, chewed up clothing of all kinds, wine corks, and all manner of items.

Clothing and string are particularly problematic. It can mean the small intestine has to be opened in several places, or worse still, a section removed completely. In addition, if the blood supply is compromised, it can result in gangrene of the area if a bowel resection is not performed. Finally, dogs will sometimes eat objects and pass them through the other end, which was the case in another sad incident I attended.

Neighbours in a nearby village looked after each other's dog when on holiday, one a Rough Haired Collie, the other a yellow Labrador. Both dogs were friendly and got on well when they were together whilst the neighbour was away.

Unfortunately, one owner looking after both dogs decided to give them some marrow bones in the back garden. Suddenly, a massive fight ensued, and the lady managed to separate them but was severely bitten in doing so. She was horrified to discover that one of her pinkies was missing, and as she was taken to hospital, a search of the garden produced nothing, proving that one of the dogs must have swallowed it. However, both dogs kept well, and the finger was never found. Sadly, the lady was an amateur classical pianist, and the accident did not help her hobby.

One of my clients was an elderly lady owning a Dachshund with chronic back problems, and unfortunately, disc trouble is commonplace in the breed. Nevertheless, she was a dear soul, obviously lonely, and insisted on me downing a sherry on every visit. I remember once remarking on an ancient and beautiful Welsh dresser in the room.

Eventually, the Dachshund was euthanised as he was aged, with the client having to go into a home. She had owned her own business in the midlands and was very intelligent, and any time I visited a client in the nearby village where the home was, I would try to pop in to see her. Sadly, she passed away before too long, and as she had no family, I was among only a few at her funeral. I was shocked a few months later when her solicitor rang to tell me that I had been left the Welsh dresser in her will.

I had the opposite experience with another elderly lady client who lived alone in a massive mansion on the edge of Yeovil. She was the last survivor of her family, and the property had hundreds of acres, a home farm, and for forty years, I visited the mansion to treat her cats. Again, she was knowledgeable, had written books, and finally became confined to bed, looked after by her lady companions.

By now, she only had one pet, an evil tempered long-haired black cat who slept on her bed all day and suffered chronic skin problems. So by now, each visit could take a long time. I had to wait outside her bedroom while her companions did her hair and make-up before I was allowed through the door to risk my fortnightly bites. The long passageway outside had a considerable collection of enormous Victorian dolls houses, which I admired as I waited patiently to see her.

She had always been very grateful for my treatment for forty years as her cats were critical to her. Sadly, she eventually passed away, and I attended her funeral (as I often did out of respect for clients I particularly liked).

At the time, I had just purchased a new car. Since the funeral was at a tiny church near her mansion, where she had been a lay reader for years, and her family were buried, the parking was very restricted, and well attended by many local dignitaries, causing chaos in the narrow lane.

On her death, I was asked to euthanise the cat by her solicitor, and the service in the packed tiny church was a fitting tribute. However, as her coffin appeared, I was amazed to see the only floral tribute on it was in the shape of a large black cat expertly represented in flowers.

When the service ended, I had great difficulty doing a four-point turn to get my new car free from the many vehicles parked closely all over the place. However, I finally succeeded, and not being used to the car, managed to hit a wall, causing several hundred pounds worth of damage to the Rover. I am sure that this was divine intervention for my hopes regarding her will, where I did not get a mention. Lesson learned!

One day a teenage girl with her father came into my consulting room with a lame rabbit. The father held it while the anxious daughter looked on. I examined the rabbit and announced that its leg was fractured. Within a second, the daughter collapsed on the floor and went into an epileptic fit. The father holding the rabbit, looked over his shoulder at his writhing daughter on the floor, turned back to me, and asked, "Can you do anything to fix the leg?"

By this time, I had forgotten the rabbit and placed blankets under the girl's head to stop her from injuring herself in the confined space. After a few minutes, she slowly recovered, and apparently, this was the first time this had ever happened. We admitted the rabbit to repair the leg and assisted the father to get his daughter safely into the car to drive her home. I advised him to keep her quiet and arrange a doctor's appointment in the next few days. I could never explain his astonishing reaction to the incident.

A few days later, a lady brought in a friendly Labrador who was scratching his ear.
It was a hot summers day, and the client was wearing a long floral dress. With her were two little girls aged about 8 and 6 who were well behaved and very concerned about their pet.

The dog was quite heavy, so I reached down and lifted him onto the table with difficulty, not realising that I had caused part of the difficulty. Somehow, in wrapping my right arm around its rear end, I had accidentally lifted part of the lady's dress, which was caught up in the dog's hindfoot.   The children burst into hysterical laughter to witness me holding the dog on the table with the dress caught in its foot and mum's underwear spectacularly exposed.   We all had a good laugh, and the younger girl could not stop giggling.

"Stop being silly, Charlotte!" admonished the older girl and received the reply, "I can't help it, Imogen!"

After treating the dog for an ear infection, I turned to the girls and asked if they had any brothers or sisters.   I was astonished when they told me they had an older brother John.
The lady was the wife of an officer at Yeovilton, and she was amazed when I told her that my three children were called John, Imogen, and Charlotte and in the same age order.

One day I was on my way to Lloyds Bank in Yeovil town centre when I saw a gentleman emerge from the bank with a briefcase and lead in his right hand. On the end of the chain lead was one of my favourite patients, a long-haired German Shepherd.

"Heidi!" I exclaimed as they neared me, knowing the spectacular response I always got when she appeared into my consulting room at work. As usual, she collapsed upside down on the pavement in front of me to have her tummy tickled. My client was a director of a large factory and went to the bank each Friday to collect cash for his worker's wages at this time each week. Unfortunately, I did not know that a padlock attached the metal lead to his briefcase containing the money. As a result, they both landed upside down on the pavement together, instead of just the dog.

Immediately a crowd surrounded him, suspecting a serious heart attack at least. At first, I had great difficulty explaining what had happened until Bert got back on his feet laughing hysterically, to the amazement and relief of the worried onlookers.

Allan and Liz Houghton were respected long-standing clients breeding beautiful, friendly Golden Retrievers. One was named Nelson, the poor soul being born with a pretty useless eye on one side. He waited excitedly for the postman's arrival every day when he would career into the hall barking loudly. Finally, the postman came to expect him and started pushing mail in and out to tease him. This only worsened his reaction, and on one occasion, he skidded on the hall floor covering and redesigned himself after going through the door window.

Allan brought him straight to my surgery, bleeding spectacularly, and fortunately, I was able to patch him up immediately, being available at their arrival.

Over the years, I have known them as friends and initially knew Allan as opening fast bowler for Sherborne. In different county leagues at the time, Yeovil and Sherborne rarely met except the occasional friendly.

Years ago, one Sunday, we did meet in a game at Yeovil, when on a damp wicket Allan's quick bowling proved quite unfriendly, as he skittled Yeovil out. But, briefly, I put up some resistance and dispatched a bouncer for six before he had his revenge! These days I still enjoy Allan's company, and as a tall lad, he is an excellent golfer, and we always enjoy our game and a good laugh together.

Another spectacular accident befell architect and local television presenter David Young, who was in his front garden. His neighbour, also a client of mine, came running down the street with his black Labrador. They had been close by starting a walk when he threw a stick which impaled in the grass, and the dog attempted to pick it up at full speed, resulting in it lodging briefly in the animal's tongue.

As they met at David's door, blood was spraying everywhere from the mouth, and David insisted that the dog and owner immediately got into his car, parked beside them. Quickly at my premises, I was lucky to have the poor Labrador anaesthetised within a minute and catch the main lingual artery with a pair of artery forceps to stop the spectacular bleeding. A few quick sutures fixed him up.

The worst casualty of the incident was David's Aston Martin, where the white roof interior lining was covered in doggie blood. However, David was only concerned about the patient, and his grateful neighbour took care of the expensive repair.

Very often, members of the public would arrive with injured birds or badgers from road accidents. Once even a young deer, so severely injured that I had to euthanise it. I then disposed of the body to not go for human or animal consumption since the remains would contain traces of the euthanasia drugs.

At one time, there was a pub in the centre of Yeovil called the Flying Machine, and the owner was a client owning two dogs, a Boxer and a German Shepherd. In the daytime, in good weather, they played in an ample open space on the roof of the building. Often the German Shepherd dog was behind the bar during the day, and one day the owner fed the Boxer alone on the rooftop. A few minutes later, he went up to check him and thought the Boxer was behaving strangely, so he rang me asking for a visit.

I attended very quickly and found the Boxer staggering all over the roof. As I watched the dog, he seemed to behave like a dog going under deep sedation, and I suddenly had an alarming thought. I asked the owner if he had fed him lately and did he have any raw meat?

The reply stunned me, as the landlord told me he had just been fed just before acting strangely and had eaten raw meat purchased from a local pet store. Fortunately, the German Shepherd dog had not yet been provided for, so I told him I suspected the flesh had probably contained some horse meat from a horse that had been euthanised with barbiturates by injection. I suggested not to use any more of the food and admitted the dog.

By the time I got to the surgery, he was unconscious, and I put him on a supportive fluid drip, plus a drug then thought to be an antagonist for barbiturate overdose. By evening the anaesthesia was so deep and breathing so slow with a cold body temperature that I thought death was imminent. We kept him wrapped in blankets with old-style hot water bags, continuous i/v fluid, and antibiotics in case of pneumonia.

Amazingly, as evening came, he started to lighten and by midnight was trying to sit up. By the next morning, he was able to go home, and the pet shop was told to investigate their supplier, which I later followed up. The owner was relieved to have the friendly Boxer back a day later.

I noticed that he was supporting the local art club, and when I returned the Boxer, I had a good look at some of the excellent work on the bar walls by local artists. The landlord showed me around, and all the paintings had a price on them. However, I was not so impressed by a large one hanging above the stairs leading to the private quarters, an example of modern art priced at £100.

A few weeks later, I visited the pub while shopping with Loraine one lunchtime, and the landlord told me that the exhibition had a lousy ending.

During the night, he was in the habit of letting the German Shepherd dog sleep in the bar for security. In the dark of the night, the weight of the painting above the stairs had been too much for the string, which had broken, causing the picture to crash to the ground and shatter the glass.

The dog had been so frightened that he had attacked the picture and tore it to pieces, miraculously not damaging himself on the broken frame and glass. Having supported the art club, the landlord now had an annoyed artist demanding £100 compensation. I have no idea of the outcome.

When kindly members of the public brought in wild animals, we tried to do what we could, free of charge, and often euthanasia was the only answer. I remember one hedgehog which had been badly injured, so I gave it an injection to end its suffering. Just then, the receptionist asked me to talk to a client at reception, so I left the poor creature dead on the table. Returning a minute later to deal with the deceased, I was horrified to see a regiment of ticks crossing the table from the dead host and fleas hopping around the room, needing fumigation with a suitable insecticide. (Rats leaving the sinking ship?).

Although many say that such parasites do not spread to dogs and cats, I have found many cases where skin trouble, especially in dogs, can magically improve when I tell owners to cease feeding hedgehogs at the end of their garden.

One hedgehog baffled me when a public member found it in a garden making a loud screaming noise. They can only be examined using gloves, as they roll into a protective ball, and often have to be given anaesthetic gas in a little box we can connect to the anaesthetic machine.

However, this particular one was moving freely on all legs and had no sign of injury.

Since I had a busy morning, I popped it into a cat pen and saw my next client as the noise continued from the recovery room.

By the time I had finished with my next patient, the screaming from the recovery room suddenly ceased, and I went to investigate. The little hedgehog was now lying happily with what appeared like three large pink raw prawns snuggled up with her.

I had never seen a newborn hedgehog before and realised the mother had been screaming in labour. However, the babies seemed active, and vestigial spines were visible, making me wonder if this made their birth painful? It made a pleasant surprise to have a happy ending for once, and the member of the public took the family back to a corner of her garden. She came in some weeks later to tell me she had watched them grow on daily inspections!

Around this time was the first charity, "Red Nose Day," so I dutifully acquired a collection box for the premises, and I alone of the staff was daft enough to wear a red nose all day. To my astonishment, not a single client commented on my appearance, and the receptionist handed in a collection to the charity, which mainly was my contribution.

One summer weekend, my former Veterinary Nurse, Alison from Rickmansworth, arrived for a weekend with her husband Tony and her family. By now, Alison had opened a kennel business at Glastonbury, boarding and breeding Shelties and German Shepherds, most of whom went to Guide Dogs or the Police, as their temperaments were outstanding.

She phoned a few days before the visit, saying a Shepherd bitch was due to have pups, and Loraine told her to bring the bitch along with the children, which she did. Our dogs did not bother about the visiting doggie, and Alison, with her husband Tony, had a rather alcoholic evening with us.

The expectant mum was installed with a vet bed in the corner of the guest bedroom. Poor Alison woke not feeling too great the following day to find a litter of puppies happily feeding in the corner of the room, encouraged by her children, our children, and some of our curious dog's peeping in the door at the squeaking babies. Happily, all was well, and after a lovely few days, the family (increased by eight) returned to Glastonbury.

My varied career brought me occasionally into contact with some famous clients, and most of them were great fun to know. For example, I was called to visit a dog in a nearby village, and at the end of a hidden drive was a massive house with lovely gardens occupied by several impressive statues.

As I was met at the door by the client's wife, I emerged from my beloved old Jaguar, and she shouted over her shoulder, "Eric! The vet has a Jag!" A short elderly gentleman arrived grinning and announced, "I used to race Jags at Brooklands before the war!" We entered through a considerable passageway into a sizeable wood-panelled hall, with statues of kilted soldiers around. The gentleman went behind a bar in one corner and entertained Loraine while his wife showed me a very old Scottish Deerhound lying on its side, breathing badly in the middle of the enormous room.

Mrs Hadcock-Mackay explained that he was deteriorating with age and had collapsed an hour ago. I examined the old dog and was sure it was the end, and treatment would appear hopeless and unwise, so I recommended the end of the line.

In the meantime, Loraine was enjoying a whisky at her husband's insistence, and he was a bit doddery. He dropped the ice on the floor, picked it up in his hand, and popped it in her glass.

She enjoyed his company, and I had to interrupt them and explain the sad decision over the much-loved Wolfhound. Then, finally, Loraine held the patient, and the old dog went off to sleep peacefully.

Afterwards, we all had a drink (mid-morning!) at the corner bar, and I learned that my host was General Eric McKay Retd. of the Parachute Regiment. During the last war, he had dropped into Arnhem in Operation Market Garden.

As a Captain at the time, he had reached the Arnhem bridge, and while John Frost held one side of the road, he was the only officer on the other side of the road, occupying the town library throughout the bridge battle with his men. Unfortunately, the situation came to a disastrous climax, and his men had held the position for several days under withering fire with many casualties. He finally had to order a retreat into the town, where he and his men fought hand to hand in back gardens, killing several Germans. He was eventually captured and had a bayonet in his backside. He spent the day with his captors before escaping again and crossing the Rhine in a stolen boat. He eventually reached the allied lines again. His brave actions with his men in holding the library for so long would probably have merited a Victoria Cross. Unfortunately, however, there was not another officer present to witness his defiant, fearless leadership.

He remained in the British Army for many years afterwards, and since they owned several animals, I always enjoyed my visits there. He was astonished to know my interest in military history and only mentioned his career when he realised I had already researched his past. However, he was happy to tell me more details of Arnhem and his fantastic escape once this was established. Like many Paras, he was small in stature, but what an amazing man, and so full of fun and kindness, and it was a privilege to have known him.

Throughout the years, I had managed to pursue my career but still have an active social life, playing cricket till age 45, gym membership, running, and in later life cycling and golf.

I played rhythm guitar, later bass guitar, and finally keyboard in four full bands, singing and playing in clubs and local music pubs for thirty years. I had some great friends through music and some wonderful times, occasionally causing surprise to some clients dancing at a function and not expecting to see their vet on stage. I was fortunate to play with some superb musicians over the years.

One friend Steve Stimpson had arrived as a child from India with tuberculosis, which blighted his life, and as a teenager, had played in Soho's famous musical Two I's coffee bar with Cliff Richard. He knew

Hank, Bruce, and other members of what was to become the Shadows. He was offered a contract to become a professional in another band. However, he turned it down because of his severe lameness due to his childhood T.B. He joined my original band, "Flying Circus," with Dave Gordon, another brilliant guitarist. The latter introduced me to the music scene.

I then switched to bass guitar with my next band, "Park Street Boys," who dominated the club scene in Yeovil for many years, with brothers Billy and Jimmy Clarke starring, and guitarist Tim Jeffries and later Alec McKay. Billy was the drummer and lead vocalist and an outrageous character, whose personality and idiotic remarks to the audience, added to a fantastic voice, guaranteed the band's success.

He was frequently at loggerheads with his brother Jimmy, an excellent guitarist, and I often ended up as peacemaker (shades of Davies brothers in the Kinks). Despite this, the band was multitalented, with great harmony singing, and on stage, we seldom stopped laughing.

I recall playing at one wedding reception when the bride was Scottish, and a coach load of kilted Scots appeared at the hotel reception. After we started to play, Billy introduced the band to many wedding guests, and when he got to me in the line-up, he announced, "Graham and I do the same job. We both cut up animals! I do it after they are dead, and Graham does it while they are still alive!"

Stunned silence ensued before he continued, "I am a butcher, and Graham is a vet!"
Inevitably, we were asked to make some Scottish dance music, and Billy announced that luckily, we had a Scotsman in the band who would oblige. So I reached in my bag for a harmonica I seldom played and announced a medley of Scottish songs to the "Gay Gordons." Before singing, I usually started with a solo on the harmonica. The first two notes I blew were fine, but the first suck brought a substantial live spider into my mouth. I spat out spindly legs as I managed to struggle through the song to the amusement of the band! "The show must go on."

I recall another wedding reception at the British Legion function room. The bride in her traditional white dress turned up for the evening function with her bridesmaids and guests. But, unfortunately, we learned that the bridegroom had failed to turn up at the altar and sent a message from Glasgow saying he was not returning. The bride accepted all her gifts and spent the evening celebrating a narrow escape. All had a good night!

I also enjoy singing with the congregation at nearby St. Michaels Church, where I have another set of friends, led by Father David and assisted by Father Chris, where there is a warm welcome for new members and children.

Even now, in retirement, I still play my solo act on a brilliant modern keyboard at a nearby small club, and Loraine and I still follow live music and do that happily with friends, usually with a beer in my hand.

My elder daughter Imogen is married to Martyn, a Squadron Leader in the New Zealand Air Force and captain of their golf team. They have lived in New Zealand for years at Palmerston North, in a lovely house in the country outside the town, with Alpacas and two dogs in their grounds, which we have visited.

Imogen keeps fit running and is a graduate, senior specialist stroke nurse, and I am very proud of both my girls working in caring professions, as does my daughter-in-law Daljit.

As I mentioned already, my sister Alison did her nurse training at the Western Infirmary in Glasgow, then midwifery at Queen Charlotte Hospital in London with several other Scottish nurses. They acquired tickets for England v Scotland at Twickenham and were given a hard time by a crowd of young England supporters in the stand behind them.

This resulted in them all going to a local pub, where one of the lads named John asked Alison for a date, and she had met her future husband! Alison ended up nursing worldwide due to John's occupation as an engineering accountant, and she ended up head of nursing at a hospital in the U.S.A. where they now live.

A few years ago, we went to the wedding of their daughter Larona near Washington. Then, one day, John opened his wallet to pay for something and showed me his ticket for the fateful day at Twickenham, which has been in his wallet for fifty years, proving the age of romance is not dead.

Charlotte lives with her husband Steve in a lovely village near Yeovil, with two teenage sons Ethan and Miles, great lads, and both bright and keen on sport. Charlotte is a lung cancer specialist sister at Yeovil District Hospital, and Steve has a business designing up-market kitchens.

With my two beautiful daughters training as nurses, I always thought that one might marry a doctor, and I was surprised when my son John married Daljit, a consultant anaesthetist. They live in Didsbury Manchester with lovely daughter Sara, very bright and a talented hockey player, playing for the regional under thirteen's. John has a tall son William from a previous marriage, now doing well as an ecology student, and he is a clone of his father.

My stepson Shaun, whom I have regarded as one of the family since he was four years old, lives now in Colchester, works in I.T. with his wife Jemma, a graduate teacher, currently working in commercial insurance. They have a son Charlie, also a clone of his dad who, has inherited his sporting abilities, and Charlie keeps goal for a junior Colchester United team. He and his lovely sister Edamay are adorable bright children.

I feel my situation is somewhat unusual at this age, with four children, all married.

My mother Kit would have been so proud of the family connections with caring professions, as was my much-loved father, Jack. He finally died in Yeovil aged ninety-seven, a miraculous age after his injuries in the second world war.

On one of our first visits to Colchester, I realised how close we were to John Constable country. I have made several visits to Dedham and Flatford Mill, where you can park at Dedham village, especially on a lovely summer's day. You can walk the mile along the River Stour as it winds with trees on its banks, swans and ducks in the water, and curious cattle around in complete peace, till you reach Flatford Mill, the scene of John Constable's famous painting "The Haywain."

Early morning no one is around, and the house of Willie Lott, Constable's friend, sits peacefully like the day of the painting. Every year, College Art students come to trim the surrounding trees, keeping them precisely as they were on the day of the picture. With my interest in art, this is a treasured favourite place for me. It is a favourite walk for Loraine and me.

While studying art at Ayr Academy, we had a written examination on art history, and I enjoyed learning so many different kinds of art over the years. However, I finally reached Vincent Van Gogh, and my interest soon became an obsession, resulting in my doing all my final examination paintings attempting his style. My art teachers were furious and surprised when I passed, and I could only surmise the examiner also liked Van Gogh.

I have twice visited Amsterdam and spent time in the marvellous museum, where most of his life's work, letters, and even his paints, palettes are preserved, and once Loraine found me in front of "The Yellow House" picture, with tears rolling down my cheeks. I get so annoyed when I hear Vincent referred to as "The mad artist who cut off his ear." It is now proved that he cut off his entire ear and survived the bleeding with no help. However, he was well educated, worked as a teacher in England, an evangelist in Belgium, wrote and spoke fluent Dutch, French and English, was a philosopher and painted most of his works in the last eight years of his life. Unfortunately, he only sold a single painting in his career. He had severe epilepsy and depression over his complete lack of success as an artist and possibly other neural problems.

He was not mad, but a sadly misunderstood genius, painted his works at great speed in eight years towards the end of his thirty-seven years without selling any, and he would have been astonished at his worldwide fame today.

Last year I went to Arles, in Provence, a town on the River Rhone, where he lived for nearly two years, part of the time with Gaugin, and painted over two hundred of his finest works. The old town is a time warp, with buildings unchanged for hundreds of years.

It was a thrill for me to walk the identical streets that Vincent did and toast him in the Cafe de la Nuit, preserved precisely like the painting, a copy of which hangs in my lounge.

The trip to Arles was a riverboat cruise, and before we went ashore at Arles, we were given a small lecture about Vincent, which ended with the playing of Don Maclean's song "Starry Starry Night" about the artist.

That night I gave the entertainments manager a copy of a song I had written and recorded about Vincent, and he played it on the boat, and it has now been added to the lecture.

I have always done some painting on my holidays. Many Greek Tavernas have my picture of the establishment on their wall, with my usual fee of an Ouzo happily supplied and the odd free meal. I calculate I have made more money from my efforts than my poor hero Vincent did!

During Covid lockdown, I have enjoyed branching into painting in landscapes in oils.

Sadly, during my career, I have acted as a witness in several R.S.P.C.A. cruelty cases.
Several of them resulted in severe penalties for appalling cruelty to pet animals, and on one occasion, to a cow.

I was delighted every time my evidence helped bring justice, though cross-examinations by barristers meant all the evidence given could be challenged minutely. For example, I recall a case involving a six-month-old Dobermann dog, which lived in a row of houses in the country. It was summertime, and the owners both worked and left the dog alone in the garden all day. The next-door neighbour noticed that the poor dog had terrible diarrhoea for several days, and by the third day, was staggering around the garden with no water on a hot day. They reported the problem to the R.S.P.C.A., who asked me to attend.

I decided the dog was suffering from viral haemorrhagic gastroenteritis and took the poor creature back to my surgery. The animal was given intravenous fluids and antibiotics and made as comfortable as possible. Unfortunately, he passed away later that day, as expected, and the Inspector asked me to carry out an autopsy. I did this in great detail, sending blood and multiple tissue samples and small intestinal contents to the laboratory.

The results agreed with my diagnosis, and it was evident that neglect was involved. The body was kept in my freezer, and after a month, I was told a court case would ensue.

Thinking over my autopsy, I decided I should have sent some large intestinal contents to the laboratory, so I repeated the autopsy and sent the further sample off.

After some months, the case finally got to court, and since the clients seemed to be not penniless, a barrister acted for the defence.
Unfortunately, however, it seemed to me that he had virtually no way of excusing the absolute neglect of the owners in not seeking veterinary help at least a day or so earlier.

The barrister made no excuses in mitigation. Instead, he built his whole defence case around the fact that I had conducted a second autopsy to take a different sample from the body. His argument centred around this fact, which he said proved that I had not done a complete autopsy in the first place and that I was therefore not competent in doing an autopsy at all. His delivery got louder, till he reached a crescendo in a style that reminded me of Adolf Hitler, ending with the words "*So*, Mr Watson, do you think you have learned something new today?" I replied with the first thing that entered my head saying, "Sir! I learn something new *every* day!"

I have no idea why that response came out. Still, the entire audience and reporters burst out laughing, and even the magistrates had difficulty disguising a smile, as the barrister's efforts failed miserably. A substantial fine and costs resulted, with a dog ownership ban for several years.

In the last year of my career, I had a call one evening asking me if I would make an evening visit to a sick German Shepherd. Since I did not recognise the name and address, I wondered if the caller was a client of mine. I was told that their usual vet had refused to visit, and I was given the name of the other practice.

Following standard protocol, I rang and spoke to the vet, who had refused the visit. He was a New Zealander and told me he had offered to see the dog if brought to his surgery premises but would not do a home visit. I pointed out that the large dog was in a state of collapse and that the owners were elderly and could not possibly lift it. Furthermore, they had no friends or relatives nearby to help and could not bring it to the surgery premises, making it his duty to do a house call.

To my surprise, he still refused to make a house call and added: "If you want to make a house visit, then carry on. I don't give a stuff!" I told him I would make the call and said goodbye.

Loraine accompanied me, and the old couple showed us the dog, completely collapsed on their lounge floor, breathing very heavily. The dog was ancient and had recently been off food and failing rapidly.

I told them he had pneumonia, probably following a stroke, and euthanasia was sadly the only option. They immediately agreed, and Loraine and I ended the poor dog's days as the old couple wept beside us. Then, with great difficulty, Loraine and I carried the heavy body and placed it in the back of my hatchback. They paid me and were very grateful.

I was horrified by the actions of the other vet and was not surprised a few weeks later to get a visit from Marie, the local R.S.P.C.A. Inspector.

She told me that the dog's owners had reported the other vet to the Royal College of Veterinary Surgeons, and I told her the dog had by now been cremated. Eventually, I had a letter from the R.C.V.S. asking me for a report since a complaint had been made against the other vet concerned. I sent off a detailed description, though I missed out on the phrase used, "I don't give a stuff!"

Some months later, when I was retired, I was advised that a case for unprofessional conduct against the other vet was to be heard at their headquarters in London and that I must attend to give evidence.

Fortunately, such cases are sporadic, but disciplinary proceedings were to be brought. Since my wife was also a witness and nurse involved, two first-class rail tickets to London were received, and our accommodation for that evening in a hotel near the R.C.V.S. Building, Belgravia House. I knew that to make sure such proceedings were fair, three disciplinary panel members were not vets, though the others were the President and high-ranking colleagues of the R.C.V.S.

On the morning in question, I arrived with some trepidation to find that the three non-vet members hearing the case included a peer, a Member of Parliament, and the President of the National Farmers Union.

The accused vet had elected not to attend, and his fate would be judged in his absence.

I was called in front of this impressive panel to give my evidence and cross-examined by the board on the veterinary detail, mainly by the vets on the panel. As I gave details of the original telephone conversation, this time I included the words spoken, "I don't give a stuff!"

Immediately the Peer picked up on the admission of this in my original written description of the evening, and he asked why my original statement did not include the phrase.

I had been expecting this to be raised. I replied that I did not expect the incident to progress to this stage when I made my initial report. I had left the phrase out initially since I was shocked and ashamed that a fellow veterinary surgeon could make such a statement.

They accepted this, and after a few more questions, the committee retired to consider the case after letters from the dog's owners were admitted as evidence since they were too old to make the journey to London.

When the panel returned, the President decided that the vet involved be struck off the list of practising Vets in the U.K. But, to my surprise, he then said that the R.C.V.S would like to commend my actions, upholding the profession's highest traditions and congratulating me on my commendable behaviour. It was a rather sad day but a relief for me that my ordeal was over, and with it, the last action of my career and justice had been done.

My last working day came in 2006, and my very last case was a terrier puppy requiring a check-over and vaccination. I told my client that this was my last case in my career since 1965 and wished he and the puppy well. The owner was pleasantly surprised when I told him that there was no fee on this particular occasion.   Loraine and I sat in the garden with a bottle of red wine in the sunshine and felt very strange at the end of an era.

Chapter Thirty-Eight
Happy Reflections

By the time I reached Rickmansworth, I was using anaesthetic machines, radiography and laboratory tests. However, I never forgot Boss Harvey's advice to use my eyes and hands to examine every inch of a patient and keep an open mind.

When I moved to Yeovil and set up my practice, I initially did not have enough money to purchase modern equipment. However, I still managed to give good service without it, sometimes relying on equipment owned by another practice on the other side of town.

Another Glasgow graduate Bill Petheram was a good friend to me. I recall calling in to see him one day, and the nurses told me to go on through to the theatre where Bill was operating. Unfortunately, he was a little short-staffed, so he asked me to scrub up and help him while we had a friendly chat.

After a little while, a drug representative stuck his head through the door, obviously hoping for a swift word when Bill had completed the surgery. But, on recognising me, a look of amazement came over his face, and Bill said, "It's only the opposition giving me a hand!"
Our friendship has survived into our retirements.

Gradually in my practice, I did acquire the equipment. The vets that I initially worked with all those years ago would be amazed to see pet animals treated with modern endoscopes, ultrasound, and sophisticated laboratory help, and the up-to-date surgical operations now possible.

My career had spanned from castrating unanaesthetised tom cats thrust into wellington boots to using all the modern equipment. My old Boss Harvey would have been astonished to watch us do pinning, plating and wiring of fractures instead of plaster of Paris as the only option.

I do like to think that proper initial examination, kindness and respect for patient and client are still the most crucial feature of the work of a vet. No two days are ever the same, and even at the end of my career, I still saw an occasional case unlike anything before in my life.

The practice I started at Wyndham Hill in 1972 now has two large branches. There is a lovely big new one on the other side of Yeovil headed by my ex-assistant, Matt Saunders. Both Mark and Matt are superb vests with excellent staff, and they have great new equipment. My ex-partner, Dr Mark Newton-Clarke, heads the other large up to date branch in nearby Sherborne.

Between them, the two ends of the practice have five vets and about twenty staff, a far cry from my opening day in my original timber premises at Wyndham Hill Yeovil in 1972.

When the Yeovil branch moved to larger premises nearly three years ago, I sold my house on Sherborne Road. Then, I converted the old surgery premises at Wyndham Hill into a modern bungalow and even closer to the beautiful hill. So, my final house move was all of fifty yards, and I now live where I worked for thirty-four years.

With the help of grandsons Ethan and Miles, we moved the furniture we intended to keep across the garden of the old house ourselves. After the boys had left, the last and most challenging item was a king-size mattress. It proved so awkward and heavy that we lost our grip and ended up on the patio with the mattress on top of us, as we laughed hysterically. Fortunately, the event was achieved quickly, and we managed to move house. Hopefully, for the last time, with no disruption to our lives, and remaining near to at least one of our children and friends, with our social life unchanged. Beautiful Wyndham Hill is now on our doorstep, to the delight of our cat, who can now spend his days chasing wild rabbits and squirrels.

The bedroom Loraine and I share used to be the operating theatre where we worked together all those years. Still, we never think about it since the new house bears no likeness to the original premises, which was reduced to a shell before being enlarged and rebuilt as a dwelling.

We were now down to two small dogs, and sadly Yorkie George, became very lame, and an x-ray for the problem showed his stifle joint destroyed by very aggressive bone cancer, which is rare in dogs, and we had to say goodbye to a much-loved naughty character. Sadly, we had to let him go, and as usual, he was not concerned about the final needle as he munched on a piece of steak.

Not long afterwards, his wife Alice, who was sixteen, and a very loveable gentle little bitch who had produced with George three litters of friendly Yorkies, developed a sudden corneal ulcer, which perforated badly within a day. So Loraine and I made the heart-breaking decision to put to sleep one of the most adorable and affectionate of our many pets. She was the last of nineteen dogs Loraine and I have owned in forty-one years.

We will never forget any of our many pets or the pleasure they have given us over the years. However, while I respect people who have no time for pet animals, they have missed out on a unique situation. It goes back to the days when our hunter-gatherer predecessors realised that dogs could be trained to help them hunt and warn of predators, animal or human, approaching them. I had even read that canine puppies developed enormous eyes when young, as this was attractive to the children of our ancestors, making ideal playmates.

We talked about our situation and decided that we would not rush into another dog since we go away frequently and have never had to leave our animals in kennels before. When I was in practice, it was always easy for one of our nurses or secretaries to move into our house while we were away, and since the dogs knew them, they were happy. However, as soon as I retired, things changed, so we made a difficult decision not to have any more pets, which fate did not like.

171

Two days after Alice died, Loraine found a kitten about four weeks old in our garden, who seemed feral. We could only assume the mother was living wild somewhere on the hill and wood behind our property, and how it got into our garden was a mystery. Loraine started to feed him, though he would spit and hiss at her and was too wild to let her go near. Finally, she slowly gained his confidence, and he slept on our patio in a cardboard box and blanket.

Inevitably, in the end, he was coaxed into the house and could be handled. We had him chipped, vaccinated, and neutered, and he is now an enormous handsome fellow with short black hair, white bib and paws. As a neutered tomcat, he is incredibly friendly. He is content to lie upside down in Loraine's arms to have his tummy tickled. The downside is a summer habit of turning up at 3 a.m., crying to let us know he has an unharmed mouse in the room with which he is playing. In my dressing gown, I usually can catch the mouse in Loraine's patent mouse catcher, an empty Pringle box, and return it to the hill behind unhurt.

The cat sleeps on the end of our bed and seems to consider us his servants. His favourite hobbies include jumping on to my Daily Telegraph as I try to read it each morning and coming from the hill in seconds of Loraine of producing chicken or beef from the oven on Sundays. I have always found cats exciting and mysterious characters if you study them. So I am not surprised that three thousand years ago in Egypt, they had a special status.

I find it difficult to believe that it is now fourteen years since I retired. Though I miss my career, I consider myself fortunate to have had such a wonderful time, trying my best for every patient, regardless of the client's financial status.

I don't miss night calls or the many bites, scratches, and kicks from my patients. All the people I worked with were friends. I was lucky with my staff, always seeming to find assistants who loved animals and were polite and kind to owners and patients. In thirty-four years of my practice, I do not remember ever giving a staff member any criticism other than suggesting a different approach in some way. We were, in effect, not a workforce but a happy family. To name but a few, both Mary's, Jill, and other girls were terrific helpers.

I find it hard to pick out an individual, but April was an outstanding helper and brilliant receptionist. She was with the practice for decades. She had a charming, sweet nature that made for an exceptional employee, and Loraine and I almost regarded her as a member of the family over the years.

April worked at Wyndham Hill until the practice moved and now lives with her retired husband Steve in a lovely country property with her horses, sheep, and miniature horses, miniature sheep and kid goats, ducks and hens. Through the local council, she now hosts visits from disabled children, both physical and mental, who feed the various animals and enjoy an exciting day.

The pleasant feeling when you have made an animal feel better, the ability to bring it into the world, or help it to leave this world painlessly, is undoubtedly a God-given privilege, and I enjoyed every moment. From 1965 onward, I witnessed enormous changes in the standard of treatment given and the massive improvements in the care. Over the years, the advances in new drugs, safer anaesthetics, sedatives, and pain relief have transformed veterinary practice to a new level of expertise.

Finally, I could never have managed most of my career without the continual love and help from my wonderful wife, Loraine. She rescued me from a dark time in my life, and has been my rock, and helped bring up our wonderful family as well, sharing many laughs and great times for forty-odd years.

Printed in Great Britain
by Amazon

74432543R00098